JAPANESE POLITICAL CULTURE

JAPANESE POLITICAL CULTURE

CHANGE AND CONTINUITY

TAKESHI ISHIDA

Transaction Books
New Brunswick (U.S.A.) and London (U.K.)

Library of Congress Catalog Number: 82-10957
ISBN: 0-87855-465-3
Printed in the United States of America

Library of Congress Cataloging in Publication Data
Ishida, Takeshi, 1923-
  Japanese political culture.
  "Bibliography of Takeshi Ishida"—p.
  Includes index.
  1. Japan—Social conditions. 2. Japan—Civilization—Occidental
influences. 3. Social values. 4. East and West. 5. Peace. I. Title
HN723.I728   1983   306'.0952   82-10957
ISBN 0-87855-465-3

*For all those who felt as I do
but did not survive World War II*

Contents

Acknowledgments

Grateful acknowledgment is made to the following publishers for granting permission to reprint previously published material:

"Elements of Tradition and 'Renovation' in Japan During the 'Era of Fascism,' " *Annals of the Institute of Social Sciences,* no. 17, 1978.

"A Current Japanese Interpretation of Max Weber," *The Developing Economies,* vol. 4, no. 3, 1966.

"Beyond the Traditional Concepts of Peace in Different Cultures," *Journal of Peace Research* (Peace Research Institute, Oslo, Norway), vol. 5, 1969.

"Japan's Changing Image of Gandhi," *Peace Research in Japan,* 1969.

"The Significance of Non-Violent Direct Action—As Viewed by a Japanese Political Scientist," *Peace Research in Japan,* 1972.

"Combination of Conformity and Competition: A Key to Understanding Japanese Society," Foreign Press Center, Tokyo, Japan.

Foreword

In recent years there has been considerable growth in the number of works on Japan by Western scholars. However, works by Japanese authors rarely appear in English, or indeed in any other European language. My *Japanese Society* (1971) was an attempt to partially fill this gap in the literature. That book sought to describe and analyze the essential features of Japanese society as perceived by a Japanese social scientist, but due to limitations of space, it could be only a brief introduction to a highly complex subject.

With the development of Japanese studies in the West, Western scholars have become more acquainted with works by Japanese scholars, written in Japanese. However, despite the fact that Japanese language materials are now fully utilized by Western scholars on Japan, the predominant trend is one of interpretation through Western eyes, rather than the actual views of Japanese scholars on their own society. In addition, until very recently even the excellent Japanese language-based research by Western scholars has been read by only a limited number of Westerners, academic or otherwise. In particular, Western scholars in the social science field who cannot read Japanese, seldom come across the works of their counterparts in Japan. Although there are some Japanese social scientists with international reputations, cultural "exchange" is still mainly in one direction, from the West to Japan. Thus in striking contrast with her economic relations, in cultural relations Japan has been importing far more than she has exported. It is the responsibility of Japanese social scientists, not only to provide sufficient information concerning Japan, but also to contribute to social sciences in general by offering an approach based upon analyses of their own society in comparative perspective. By doing so it may also contribute to improving the level of social science analysis regarding other non-Western societies.

In 1979 Professor Irving Louis Horowitz of Rutgers University came to see me, and while we were talking I showed him my list of publications. Then, at his request, I sent him copies of all my articles in English. He responded by proposing that I publish a collection of my essays. His offer was most generous and I was given complete freedom concerning the selection of essays. Moreover, there was no limit on the

ix

number of pages. By chance, Mr. Ian Gow, a Ph.D. candidate at Sheffield University, came to Japan as a research fellow at our Institute of Social Science, University of Tokyo. He kindly offered his assistance in preparing the book, not only by correcting my English, but also by advising on the selection of articles. After examining all the articles, we reached our conclusions based on the following principles of selection. First, those articles easily available in English, such as those published in major academic journals or books in the United States or the United Kingdom would not be included. Secondly, articles written in Japanese, specifically for a Japanese readership and later translated, should not be included. Thirdly, articles of interest only to the Japan specialist—for example, biographical essays on important modern Japanese figures such as Yukichi Fukuzawa and Kanzō Uchimura— ought to be excluded. In a more positive sense it was then decided that the articles be structured in such a way that social scientists not specializing in Japan, or with only a minimum background knowledge on Japan, would find them both interesting and informative. Finally, continuity and change in modern Japan was to be the main theme and the value system and the organizational structure were to be the principal focal points.

Regarding continuity and change, it is necessary to identify both the traditional and the new elements. Those two often seemed synonymous with the Eastern and the Western elements. Of course, "East" is not a homogeneous entity, being composed of such diverse cultures as those of India, China, and so on. More precisely, one ought to use terms such as "non-Western" in order to clarify the focal points selected for emphasis. Chapter one was specially written as a general introduction for the book, and chapter four "Westernism and Western 'Isms' " was also written specifically for this volume. Out of more than twenty articles so far written (a list of these is included in the bibliography), six were chosen to form a major part of the book. Mr. Gow kindly went through each chapter carefully for readability. Considerable effort was made to avoid overlapping but sometimes this proved impossible because certain events were mentioned in different contexts. The result of this process is the present volume.

The general introduction (chapter one) identifies continuity and change in modern Japan, chapter two deals with the particular combination of conformity and competition, with an emphasis on continuity. In part II there are case studies which, one hopes, will shed light on various aspects of modern Japan in comparative perspective: Chapter three deals with methodological problems by utilizing Japanese scholars' interpretations of Max Weber as a case study. The problem of

East and West is treated in the next chapter against the general background of the Japanese intellectual climate. Chapter five is a detailed case study of "the era of fascism" in Japan again with emphasis on the comparative perspective, in this case with Germany.

Part III is also related to the principal focal points of this book, but since the three articles included here were all in the field of peace research, they formed a separate section. The first article is a comparative study of the concepts of peace in different cultures in order to characterize Japan's traditional concept of peace. The next chapter is a case study of the Japanese image of Gandhi, which also offers certain cross-cultural comparisons. The final chapter deals with a specific subject, nonviolent direct action, which is closely related to the author's personal value commitment. In order to give the reader a better understanding of this point and the overall value premise which underlies the entire volume, I should like to add something of my personal experience.

Let me briefly explain the motivation and historical development of my research. First it is necessary to touch on my experience during the war, although that period actually precedes my research career. When General Tōjō became prime minister in 1941, he declared that the years of study for high school would be shortened to two and one-half instead of three years. Thus we had to finish our high school days half a year earlier than expected. Moreover, he also declared in 1943 that university students in the humanities and social sciences were no longer exempt from military service; I was conscripted into the army that year and served until Japan's defeat in 1945. When I returned to my studies at the University of Tokyo, what interested me most was why we had been so deeply indoctrinated by ultranationalism that we had never questioned the cause of the war. This interest was the result of serious reflection on my wartime experience, rather than mere academic curiosity. In order to establish my own identity in the completely changed value orientation of the period immediately after the defeat, it was imperative to find the answer as to why I had succumbed so easily to Japan's ultranationalist ideology.

My determined search for a new identity resulted in a decision to become a social scientist in order to discover what had been the fundamental cause of the widespread ultranationalist ideas during the last war. First, I focused attention on the system of moral education based upon the Imperial Rescript on Education of 1890, because, judging from my personal experience, it was one of the most important means of ultranationalist indoctrination. While I was tracing the historical development of moral education, I came across the important epoch in the late Meiji period, around 1911, when the "family-state" idea was formed.

In my analysis, the family-state idea historically contained two elements. The first was a traditional familism buttressed by Confucian ethics. The familism, which included the extended family system, was expanded to cover the whole nation in such a way that the imperial family was considered to be the main family for all Japanese families. Another element was the organic theory of the state introduced from the West, particularly from Germany. The organic theory of the state, partly corresponding to the newly established bureaucratic system, was important in displacing the ideas of popular sovereignty and natural law advocated by the activists in "people's rights" movements in the late 1870s and the early 1880s. In my first book, in Japanese, *Studies in the History of Meiji Political Thought* (1954), which I finished at the end of my period as an assistant at the Faculty of Law, University of Tokyo, under the supervision of Professor Masao Maruyama, I wanted to explain the process of the formation of the family-state idea together with its ideological structure and its actual functioning in Japanese society. The familistic element in the family-state idea had proved useful in mobilizing the personal sentiment found in the family relationship and applying it to loyalty to the state. At the same time, the organic theory of the state was important in justifying the existing law and social order.

After this first book, my interest was expanded in two directions: first, it became broader, covering not only the history of political thought but also political history; second, the period under consideration was extended to cover not only the Meiji period, but also the entire modern period (1868 to the present). Thus in my second book in Japanese, *Studies in the Political Structure of Modern Japan* (1956), I dealt with the constitution, local government, bureaucracy, and party politics in modern Japan.

When I started work at the Institute of Social Science, University of Tokyo, I began field surveys of both rural and urban Japan, including one of election campaigning and local politics. Maintaining my original motivation, my interest focused on Japanese politics in its historical context as well as in comparative perspective.

I paid particular attention to the organizational structure as well as to the symbols used for the integration of organizations. While analyzing agricultural cooperatives in rural areas and labor unions in urban areas, I found one important characteristic common to both. It was a dual structure composed of a highly bureaucratized body in the upper strata and a basic unit at the bottom where a naturally developed sense of conformity existed among those who were living or working together. (In the case of a Japanese labor union, it is based upon the enterprise; the custom of lifetime employment allows the same workers to work together until their retirement. This structure is related to the particular characteristic of symbols used for the integration of the organization. There is a tendency toward "replacement of goal,"—i.e., "forgetting" the specific goal for which the organization was established; mere identification with the organization becomes the goal. In this sort of organization, integration can easily be obtained by strengthening the existing sense of conformity in the basic units, which is then mobilized for the members' identification with the whole organization. At the same time, however, because of the lack of a clear understanding of the specific goal for which the organization was established, there tends to be an indifferent attitude toward this goal; this indifference becomes a serious bottleneck hindering the spontaneous and active participation of the members.

In my book in Japanese, *Contemporary Organization* (1961) I dealt with this problem and offered a general theory based upon a concrete analysis of contemporary organizations in Japan. Japanese organization can be considered unique in one respect, but if we consider the problem of informal small groups in huge organizations and the problem of personal influence of subleaders in many other societies, the Japanese case may well be only an extreme example of an aspect of all contemporary organizations in mass society. That was precisely why I attempted to establish a general theory of contemporary organizations based upon my analysis of Japanese organizations.

While *Contemporary Organization* was a product of my study in the field of sociological theory and the analysis of contemporary society, my interest in political history continued and, moreover, I extended the latter to include more recent history. *An Analysis of the Political Process in Japan from 1941 to 1952* was the result. This study was an effort to combine political science analysis and a historical approach to the period from the beginning of the Pacific War to the end of the Occupation. The Japanese title *Catastrophe and Peace* indicated that my motivation at the beginning of my career still continued. Although this book was published in 1968 due to delays on the part of other authors in the same series, I actually finished writing it before I went to the United States in 1961, my first experience abroad.

While I was in high school we studied German twelve hours a week and English for only one hour. This was of course partly due to it being the period of the Axis alliance. I spent my university days and the early part of my career under the Allied Occupation. Since I felt very uncomfortable watching many Japanese flattering (or so I perceived it) American GIs by speaking English, I purposely did not speak any English during the period of the Occupation. Of course, for academic reasons I read books written in English, but my deep interest in Max Weber, G.W.F. Hegel, Karl Marx and Georg Lukács made me feel more comfortable in German. At the time of the political crisis in 1960 brought about by the revision of the security treaty between the United States and Japan, however, I felt it necessary to communicate with my American colleagues in order to improve their understanding of the Japanese situation. My opinions were published (the first time in English) in "The Diet Majority and Public Opinion," *Far Eastern Survey* 29:10 (October 1960) but this was translated from the Japanese. At any rate, my wish to communicate with American colleagues was realized when I was awarded a Rockefeller Foundation grant to study in the United States.

I stayed at the University of Michigan, Ann Arbor, the University of California, Berkeley, and Harvard University in Cambridge, Massachusetts, for a period of two years. At the beginning I found it extremely difficult to communicate in English, but the fact that I was exposed to a different culture gave me a tremendous academic stimulus. The difficulty in communication made me even more aware of the difference in culture. With the kind arrangement of my American colleagues, such as Robert E. Ward, I was invited to participate in various academic conferences, such as on "Political Development and Bureaucracy," "Modernization in Turkey and Japan," "Political Development in Modern Japan," all sponsored by the Social Science Research Council. At that time the theory of political modernization dominated comparative politics in the United States. I found it to be an interesting attempt to find more objective indices for comparison, eliminating the fixed ideological dichotomy beween the free democratic world and the totalitarian communist world. At the same time I was not entirely satisfied with modernization theory because of its assumption of a unilinear type of development computed by per capita income, percentage of actual voters, etc. To me, what was more important was the *pattern* (rather than the degree) of development related to the problem of culture. I touched on this briefly in my article "The Development of Interest Groups and the Pattern of Political Modernization in Japan," in R. E. Ward (ed.), *Political Development in Modern Japan,* (1968).

My study in the United States and my contact with such scholars as R. Bellah, T. Parsons, D. Riesman and S. N. Eisenstadt (then a visiting professor at Harvard University) broadened my interest and made me more oriented towards comparative studies. Although I had previously focused on Japan, I now started to examine Japanese culture in a broader context.

My first concrete attempt to develop this idea was realized when I published *Politics for Peace* (1968); an English summary of the first part of that book appeared in an article, "Beyond the Traditional Concepts of Peace in Different Cultures" (1969, chapter six of this volume). As the reader can see from that article, I tried to characterize the traditional concept of peace in Japan compared with similar concepts in different cultures.

Politics for Peace indicates two further developments in my research interests: peace research and studies of important concepts in particular political cultures. In the field of peace research, "Japan's Changing Image of Gandhi" (chapter seven), and "The Significance of Non-Violent Direct Action—As Viewed by a Japanese Political Scientist" (chapter eight) are examples of the former. My *Logic of Peace and Social Change* (in Japanese, 1973) was an attempt to show how the conservatism of peace *maintenance* should be supplemented by peace *building* so as to overcome the "structural violence" in society.

My interest in the variety of political concepts among cultures can be seen in my essay on the introduction of various Western concepts, such as those of "freedom" and "right," into Japan ("The Assimilation of Western Political Ideas and the Modernization of Japan," 1980). Because the traditional concepts in Japan did not correspond exactly to the Western concepts, new terms had to be found to translate these words. Thus the contact between different political cultures provides us with an interesting problem reflecting on both cultures. It is not simply the problem of acculturation or cultural assimilation on the part of the receiving (or 'peripheral') culture. As Max Weber pointed out, it may also be an opportunity to question the meaning of the donor (or "central") culture. Center-periphery theory among peace researchers, such as Johan Galtung, may be directly related to this problem.

After the United States started the bombing of North Vietnam, I ceased visiting the U.S. in protest. Instead, I accepted an invitation to teach at El Colegio de Mexico in 1971 and 1972. As a reflection of my experience in Mexico, I published *Mexico and the Japanese* (in Japanese, in 1972) with the subtitle *Observations from the Third World*. When the war in Vietnam was over, I accepted an invitation to teach at the University of Arizona in 1976 and 1977. It was my first experience of living in the southwest of the United States, and by making contact with Mexican Americans and Native Americans I found another view of the United States, rather different from that of the intellectuals on the east coast. It was in a sense the view from the periphery. Thereafter I visited Tanzania to teach for a semester in 1978; I also visited China and other third world countries, because I wanted to know more about the view of the world held by those in the Third World.

To return to the methodological problem, my discontent with certain aspects of the American political scientists' theories of comparative politics in general and the theory of political modernization in particular resulted in my increased interest in political culture. I wanted to make the best use of my career as a historian on the one hand, and a social scientist on the other, and to analyze political culture in Japan in both historical and comparative perspectives. *Japanese Society* (1971) was a result of that effort, although it was merely a brief introduction, a sort of bird's-eye view. Writing something introductory in a foreign language, within a limited space, was very frustrating and I wanted to write more freely in Japanese on the same subject. *Japanese Political Culture: Conformity and Competition* (in Japanese, 1970) was a product of this effort. An English summary of this book appeared in English as a booklet, *Combination of Conformity and Competition: A Key to Understanding Japanese Society* (1980); this was modified and incorporated into the present book as chapter two.

My experience of teaching at the University of Arizona with the excellent historian Gail Bernstein; in Oxford, England at seminar with Richard Storry, one of the most respected European scholars on Japan, and with others, has made me more oriented towards history in an effort to cancel out the schematic approach which permeates political science. The two key disciplines in my research, political science and history, continuously engage in conflict in my mind. This conflict is not necessarily disadvantageous. I have been hoping that it can and should be utilized as a driving force to produce a creative result. *Law and Politics in the History of Modern Japanese Thought,* (in Japanese, 1976), a collection of articles written over the past twenty years, represents my efforts in the field of history. My most recent publication in Japanese, *Organizations and Symbols in Contemporary Politics: A Political Scientist's View of Postwar Japan,* (1978), is an effort to combine my approaches as political scientist and historian.

As the Japanese economy grows rapidly and as Japan has become an economic superpower, national self-confidence is also growing. Japan's economic development is now rated highly by American experts on modernization. I have, however, maintained a critical view of Japanese society. This is because the problem still remains as to why Japan possessed no internal forces capable of changing the political system from within until Japan was defeated by the Allied forces and forced to introduce the reforms ordered by the Occupation authorities.

Among my American colleagues, voices critical of liberal Japanese intellectuals have been heard saying that Japanese intellectuals are too critical of their own society. I would admit that this may be true, but in my view there are sufficient and good reasons for our being so critical. Despite the rapid changes taking place in Japanese society, there are certain prewar elements, such as the strong attitudes of conformity and competition still found in the post-war period. History may not repeat itself, but we cannot ignore historical continuity.

Some may criticize me for being a dreamer because of my commitment to pacifism. No one, however, except for opportunists, can be competely free from any value commitment. What is important is to be aware of one's value commitment in order to avoid possible biases due to the wishful thinking based on that commitment. A dreamer is a person seeking an impossible goal without due consideration of the actual situation, whereas an idealist in the strict sense, is a person who is seeking an ideal goal based on a realistic analysis of the actual situation. My hope is that by maintaining a critical view of my own society I can contribute to improving it by a careful scientific investigation of it. Of course, my wish to be an idealist with a realistic approach may itself be a dream, a piece of wishful thinking. How far I have achieved this must be judged by what I have written so far.

When I consider my academic career up to the publication of this volume, I cannot but reflect on my great fortune in receiving academic stimuli from various distinguished scholars both in Japan and abroad. Professor Masao Maruyama, whose seminar I attended from its very beginnings in 1946, is the person to whom I owe my greatest debt. Professor Kiyoaki Tsuji and other political scientists in the Law Faculty of the University of Tokyo have greatly influenced and stimulated me through various seminars. Colleagues in the Institute of Social Science, University of Tokyo have proved of great help during our work on various common projects. In the West, the names of scholars mentioned above are merely a few examples from among many. I would like to express my heart-felt gratitude for their kind help and valuable suggestions.

Related to the publication of this volume, the first person whom I would like to thank is Professor Irving Louis Horowitz. Without his kind offer and continued encouragement, I might not have dared to attempt to publish another book in English. *Japanese Society* required so much effort that I felt that one was quite enough. Mr. Ian Gow, who spent a great deal of his time on this volume, deserves particular acknowledgement. Without his advice and help, this volume would have been a mere collection of old essays lacking any structure. In terms of style too, he helped considerably in rewriting various essays which had originally been written, and often translated, with the help of different persons. The various translators of my Japanese manuscripts deserve special thanks, especially my colleague, Mr. Fumiaki Moriya, an assistant of our institute. I am thankful also to those who helped me with the original essays. I appreciate Professor Patricia G. Steinhoff's assistance in the process of proofreading.

I am also grateful to Mr. Kinji Kawamura, the president of the Foreign Press Center, the editors of *The Journal of Peace Research, Developing Economies, Peace Research in Japan* and *Annals of the Institute of Social Science of the University of Tokyo* for their generosity in granting me permission to use my essays previously published in their journals.

T.I.
Tokyo, Japan

Part I

GENERAL INTRODUCTION

CHAPTER ONE

Basic Characteristics of Modern Japan: Value System and Social Structure

I. Introduction

Recently Japanese intellectuals have been puzzled by the high evaluation, in both the East and the West, of Japan's modern development: from the United States, the enemy during World War II, later the principal power in the Occupation of Japan and the most important in the modernization of postwar Japan; and from mainland China, against whom Japan had been engaged in hostilities from the 1880s until the end of World War II. If we recall the predominant image of Japan in those countries one generation ago, this change is quite remarkable. Then, the predominant American image was that of a country still in the process of rehabilitation from semifeudalism and militarism, whereas the Chinese image of Japan was that of "a running dog of American imperialism." Those two images were, in a sense, in opposition. Any balanced evaluation of modern Japan must seek to explain what made possible such opposite assessments. This will be done here. What is attempted is an analysis and evaluation of Japan's modern development from a Japanese social scientist's viewpoint.

In the parts which follow the development of modern Japan will be divided into two stages: the first, from the Meiji Restoration (1868) to the end of World War II; and the second, from the defeat of Japan in World War II up to the present. Two approaches will be used: the first is an investigation of the essential features of the modern Japanese value system, which comprises both traditional and new elements; the second is the investigation of organizational structure, which also is composed of traditional and new elements. In this way, historical continuity and change can be viewed in a balanced way. Also, since the new elements correspond approximately to Western elements, if one can find the pattern of combination of traditional and new elements both in value system and organizational structure, this helps to also identify the Western influence and the way it was modified to suit Japanese society. In this way Japan's modern development will be considered both from the perspective of uniqueness and from the features common to Western societies.

II. The Period between 1868 and 1945

Value System

If we look at the first stage of modern development we see two core values: the first, a strong tradition of group cohesiveness; the second, a national goal which drove the leaders of the newly reorganized Japanese nation-state: "To catch up with and surpass the Western powers."

The traditional value system in Japanese society prior to the Meiji Restoration requires detailed explanation, but a brief summary must suffice here. Western tradition—both Judeo-Christian and Islamic—bases its value orientation on its belief in a transcendent God; whereas in both Chinese and Japanese societies transcendental values are lacking—or rather values are based upon and fused with the worldly order. To put it another way, values are principally centered on the maintenance and furtherance of the *group*.

Within the same immanent type of value orientation, there is a difference between China and Japan even though both share the same Confucian tradition. In China, although a transcendental value is lacking, some universalistic ideas such as that of *t'ien* (heaven) clearly exist. In fact, if the mandate of heaven changed (i.e., if the government lost its legitimacy) it was cause for revolution. (The Chinese expression for revolution literally means "change of the mandate of heaven.") This idea was used, in effect, to justify the change of dynasty after it had taken place, but the fact remains that there was an ethical and cultural provision for such a justification. In contrast, the idea of a change in the mandate of heaven never took root in Japan. When the Confucian classics were introduced in Japan this idea was carefully avoided, because Japanese Imperial rule had no other source of legitimacy than the belief that it had existed from the very beginnings of history. In this sense, the Chinese traditional value system was more universalistic and the Japanese one more particularistic, although they both existed within the same category of immanent value orientation.

Although group cohesiveness continued to be the same after the Meiji Restoration, the size of the group changed. Under the Tokugawa shogunate the *han* (fief) was the major focus of loyalties, but as a result of the Western impact the sense of nationality became stronger, and with the reorganization under the new Meiji government the focus of loyalties shifted to the state. Of course this shift did not take place overnight. It is true that there had already been some potential for a national consciousness before the restoration; under the Tokugawa regime there had been a network of communication and transportation throughout the nation, and there had always been a vague sense of national identity. On the other hand, after the civil strife connected with the restoration, it took some time to establish a more solid, i.e., politically effective, sense of national identity.

One contributory factor among traditional elements in establishing a national identity was the familism mobilized to create the family-state idea. The Japanese traditions of ancestor worship and subordination of branch families to the main family were integrated to achieve loyalty on a national scale. The imperial family was regarded as the main family of the entire Japanese people, and the nation regarded as an extended family: The emperor occupied the position of patriarch of the common main family.

In addition to the above, a strong impetus for the establishment of loyalty to the nation appeared after the Meiji Restoration. It was a goal formulated under the impact of the ships and cannons of the Western powers which had compelled Japan to open her doors to the world. The slogans, "Maintain independence," "Catch up with and surpass the West," and "A rich nation and a strong military" reflected such national goals, and Japan commenced rapid modern development based on a broad national consensus. Generally speaking, it may be better to deal with a national goal as a matter of policy rather than of value; but in the case of Japan, because of the immanent nature of value orientation and the strong tradition of group cohesiveness once the national goal is decided, the goal becomes internalized in popular mind to form a part of value itself. Since the goal to catch up with and surpass the Western powers was considered imperative for the maintenance of national independence, this goal occupied a major role in the national value system.

The goal to catch up with and surpass the West was considered so important that anything which was useful for the achievement of this goal was used without hesitation. The lack of transcendental religion in Japan proved advantageous here. There was no need for secularization, as in Turkey prior to the introduction of Western institutions and ideas. Compared with China, where transcendental religion was also lacking, Japan proved more flexible in accepting Western ideas. In China, partly because of its more universalistic, yet static Confucianism and its self-image as the "central empire," it proved more difficult to accept Western ideas. (The Chinese term for their own nation, *chung kuo,* means "central empire," an idea originally more cultural than political.) The different vehicle for Confucian ethics in the two countries was also related to the difference in flexibility. The Chinese bureaucrats were literati who had passed the difficult civil service examination on the Confucian classics. The Tokugawa bureaucrats, who were originally *samurai* (warriors), assumed both civil and military responsibility, whereas in China authority over military matters rested chiefly in the hands of the more-or-less autonomous warlords. The Tokugawa bureaucrats, as warriors, were pragmatic and placed great importance on the ability to deal with any contingency. Despite their comparatively low hierarchical position under feudalism, those *samurai* who possessed practical administrative skills and the ability to deal with the outside world (many had dealt with, or studied with, the Dutch traders) became increasingly influential. Once the seclusion policy was abolished and the policy of westernization was officially decided they were able to lay the groundwork for rapid development.

Among the various Western ideas important in the context of this chapter was Social Darwinism, which began to spread rapidly in Japan from the 1880s. Hiroyuki Katō, president of Tokyo University 1877–1886, had been one of the key figures in bringing the Western concept of natural law into Japan in the early years of Meiji. But Katō soon ceased to advocate this concept and, in 1882 published his *Jinken Shinsetsu (New Theory of Human Rights)* in which he insisted that the Western concept of natural law, with its emphasis on the natural rights of man, was nothing but an "illusion" and that Social Darwinism was the only theory that revealed the truth about man and society. In Katō's *Kyōsha no Kenri no tame no Tōsō (The Struggle for the Rights of the Strong,* 1893), he developed Social Darwinism into an ideology that justified the domination of the weak by the strong.

However, Katō argued that, in order to avoid being replaced by an even stronger group of men, the ruling class must not permit open competition for survival to continue for too far. He insisted that even if seen only from the point of view of a national conformity which sets a high value on "harmony," unrestricted internal competition for survival should not be tolerated. Katō recognized competition only in the realm of international relations, and he advocated the organic theory of the state in the domestic area. Briefly, what Katō came to espouse, from around the turn of the century, was the notion that the state was an organism whose head—which corresponded to the ruling class of the society—could not be "removed," for that would kill the organism. Katō observed that, in contrast to this idealized situation, the conditions that prevailed in the actual world were those of dog-eat-dog, which he attributed to the backwardness of the world order. In effect, Katō saw strife and competition as a means for achieving ultimate stability.

One additional point must be made concerning Social Darwinism: the difference in the roles that it played in Japan and China. Social Darwinism became popular in China at the end of the 1890s when Yen Fu and others introduced the concept. Its popularity lasted much longer than in Japan, and in 1907 Lu Hsün translated into Chinese a study by Ernst H. Haeckel, who also had been instrumental in converting Katō from natural law to Social Darwinism. While Japan's Social Darwinists considered Japan as a country rapidly joining the ranks of the powerful in the international arena, the Chinese intellectuals who espoused the concept of Social Darwinism could not, considering the weakness of the Chinese position in the world, help but argue that open competition for survival was a process that denied the existence of the weak. Therefore, in place of Social Darwinism, with its emphasis on the importance of competition for survival, many Chinese intellectuals came to favor either Kropotkin's anarchism with its advocacy of a system of mutual aid or the Marxist theory of the class struggle.

As Marxism became popular among Japanese intellectuals from the 1920s, it came to completely overshadow Social Darwinism. After it had successfully discredited the idea of natural law, Social Darwinism was rapidly replaced by Marxism on the left wing of the political spectrum, and by the organic theory of the state in all other areas to the right. Although Social Darwinism as a theory was very short-lived, the idea behind it continued to survive in the minds of the masses, particularly as a rationale for the idea that "might is right" internationally.

Organizational Structure

In terms of social structure also, new features were fused with traditional elements. Corresponding to the traditional value, i.e., group cohesiveness, the traditional element in the social structure was the homogeneous, conformist in-group, the basic unit of the society. Since the Japanese people from early times settled and grew rice on what little land they had, it is hardly surprising that conformist in-groups were formed in rural communities. Villagers had to work together very closely during specific periods when a large work force was needed—

such as for the gathering of grass for fertilizing and feeding livestock, the securing of irrigation water, the transplanting of rice, and of course harvesting. After the restoration too, so long as the production of rice continued to employ the majority of the population, the village structure managed to survive the rapid political and social changes.

When the Meiji leaders took measures to establish a centralized government, the villages were incorporated as subunits within the prefectures that had replaced the old *han* as the administrative divisions of the central government. One of the important reasons for the Meiji leaders establishing a system of local government even before they formed the national parliament (Diet) was that they wanted to mitigate the escalating conflict between the government and the infant political parties by emphasizing the conformity which existed in village life.

Based upon the above-mentioned rural communities, Meiji leaders built up a bureaucratic structure of government which was a new element extensively introduced into Japan from the West. Although a semicentralized form of government already existed in the Tokugawa period, administrative power was in the hands of the hereditary *samurai* (warrior/ bureaucrat) class. When bureaucratic organization was introduced from the West together with the Western legal system, the Meiji leaders wished to recruit personnel for the bureaucracy based upon ability rather than family background. Thus an examination system for civil officials was introduced in 1887. It is interesting to note that in China the old type of examination system, based upon the ability to memorize Confucian classics, survived until as late as 1904; it therefore proved more difficult in China to introduce western types of bureaucratic organization than in Japan.

By a bureaucratic type of organization, is meant here a public or private organization established for a specific goal, composed of members recruited by achievement rather than ascription, and subject to a set of rules based on functional division of labor. Civil and military bureaucracies and business organizations belong to this category and all form indispensable elements in modern society. In this sense the introduction of bureaucratic organization as a new element from the West is not peculiar to Japan. What is of considerable importance here is the precise relationship between the traditional element and this new element in the social structure.

Generally speaking, the relationship between the two elements in Japan is much closer and much more continuous than in many other societies. If we make a comparison with China—where, like Japan, the family and the rural community have long been the prototypes and basic units of social organization—we see that in Japan the family and community played a centripetal role vis-à-vis the central government, whereas their function in China was centrifugal. In other words, there was a greater gulf between family/community and central government in China than in Japan. In terms of shared Confucian ethics, in China filial piety was given priority over loyalty to the state or emperor while in Japan the opposite was the case. The reason for this difference is complex, and difficult to explain. One element is the different degree to which the central power penetrated down to the grass-roots level. In traditional China central government was not only physically but also psychologically remote from the daily life of the common people and so long as their daily family and community life were not interfered with, the common people were rather indifferent as to who governed the country. This was partly because the central government's bureaucratic administrators had no real contact with the people in the communities other than in the collection of taxes. In traditional Japan, however, the relationship between the local ruler and peasants had grown closer, with an accompanying psychological attachment. This was partly due to the smaller size of the country with its better network of communication and transportation, but chiefly it was because the relationship had continued uninterrupted for several centuries.

At the time of the Restoration the old *han* (fief) was abolished and was replaced by the prefecture, an administrative unit headed by a governor appointed by the central government. In this way, although the personal ties between the feudal lord and the rural community were eliminated, the sense of the *han* remained. The leaders of the newly established government tried to link the central government with the traditional village community so that the sense of unity and conformity could be extended to the national level. Conflict between local units could then be avoided by enlarging the in-group unit to absorb, and thus pacify, the conflicting parties.[1]

Development

So far the traditional and new elements in both value system and social structure have been identified; Also the relationship between the old and new elements at the beginning of the modern period was briefly mentioned. Although the emphasis has so far been on integration, it is also true that the old traditional elements and the new elements were often in conflict with each other, because the latter were, or were considered to be, Western elements and hence alien in the eyes of conservative Japanese: When the goal of industrialization was being encouraged by the state bureaucracy, the human relationships in the newly established factories were seen as very different from those in rural communities. The introduction of a Western legal system was feared to be a threat to the old morals and customs. Bureaucracy was seen as too impersonal, or even inhuman.

These were not simply fears, as industry developed and urbanization inevitably threatened the closed in-group that is dominant in the rural communities. Two remedies were prepared: One was the strong emphasis on the familistic aspect of the family-state, so as to ease the antipathy toward the state apparatus—this was particularly notable in moral education. The second was the government's encouragement of local initiative, exemplified by the subsidizing of semivoluntary and semigovernmental associations (e.g., agricultural, women's, youth's and reservists' organizations). These two related policies emerged near the end of the Meiji period (1912) to help the people adjust to the accelerating urbanization and to relieve the anxieties of the traditional rural population. These measures were not simply a passive adjustment to the changing situation, but a more positive attempt to broaden and consolidate the social basis of bureaucratic organization by mobilizing semivoluntary organizations. In terms of value, too, "a harmony of Eastern and Western civilizations" was emphasized to ease the tension between the two.

It was not difficult for politicians, such as Shigenobu Ōkuma (prime minister 1898–1911 and 1914–16) to propose the idea of a harmony of Eastern and Western civilizations, but it was quite another matter to realize this idea in a concrete social situation. As rapid urbanization took place there was an accumulated resentment among the people in rural areas, who felt they were not only being left behind but were being sacrificed to rapid industrialization; for example, their land taxes were diverted for the promotion of rapid industrialization. In the eyes of rural people the industrialization and urbanization that were threatening the old way of life were created by Western contact. Thus the tensions between urban and rural areas were inextricably entangled with those between East and West, and leads to the problem of ultranationalism.[2]

The situation in rural areas became particularly serious when the economic crisis of 1929 hit Japan and popular disturbances threatened the stability of many rural communities. Efforts were made to restore order in the villages: Large landowners and absentee landlords were restrained from making excessive profits, while those independent farmers and land owners who cultivated their own land were placed at the center of village life where they could take an active part in cooperatives and help to restore "conformity" to the rural communities.

Although, in the view of peasants, urban areas were contaminated by Western influence, the situation in the factories was not fully Western. Members of the urban working class, mostly second and third sons of farming families, maintained ties with native villages as places to return to in case they lost their jobs or retired, and where they would be buried. Indeed, the government, aware of the traditional ties, actually formulated a policy of sending unemployed workers back to their home villages in the 1930s.[3] As industrialization progressed, however, the workers came to feel more and more estranged from their village, which ironically heightened their nostalgia for traditional village life. It was not difficult for the government and management to take advantage of such a situation and transform the relationship between management and workers into a pseudo–parent-child relationship just as it had similarly transformed the relationship between landowners and tenant farmers. The government thus created an ideology of "enterprise-family" that served to mitigate the conflict between labor and management. This emphasis on the enterprise as a family was later institutionalized in the form of a campaign to encourage cooperation between labor and management called the *Sangyō Hōkokukai* or *Sampō* (Associations for Service to the State through Industry).[4] In this way the state, as one big family, incorporated the enterprises into its household as subsidiary families. As ultranationalism accelerated, everything related to the West (except for certain German elements), from social science to the arts, was rejected.

It is interesting to note that Western ideas such as Oswald Spengler's *Decline of the West* (*Der Untergang des Abendlandes*, 1918) and that of German Nazism, were utilized by the Japanese rightist intellectuals simply as a means of criticizing Western civilization, particularly liberalism and communism; when they had served their purpose of criticizing the West, they were replaced by traditional ideas. Although Western technology was fully used for the goal of total war, fanaticism and an irrational belief in *kamikaze* (God's wind) resulted in the suicide plane tactics.

Evaluation

If we agree that Japan's modern development was characterized by the features that I have so far outlined, what then were the positive and the negative aspects of the modernization of Japan in the period from the Meiji Restoration to the end of World War II?

First, on the positive side, we must cite the attainment of rapid industrialization and the building of a rich nation and a strong military through the united efforts of the people. In response to outside pressure, group-oriented values manifested themselves in the form of nationalism. The people's strong sense of unity as a nation made it possible for the Japanese to introduce Western technology freely, without any fear of losing their integrity as a people. Because no tradition of faith in one transcendental God existed, there was a strong tendency to orient the religious consciousness of the Japanese toward secular goals. That is, there was nothing in the Japanese experience, from the viewpoint of traditional religious expression, that was notably in opposition to Westernization; there was no need to contradict religious values and insist that the precondition for modernization be secularization. Not only that, but the traditional values transmitted in Japanese agricultural society placed a premium on organic growth; the soil was fertile indeed for the implantation of Social Darwinism from the West.

Consequently, competition with the Western powers and competition within Japan for social advancement could be justified in terms of an existing system of values. The bureaucratic system that had been adopted as a method of social organization played an important role in the promotion of state-guided industrialization; private industry gradually developed as private capital was accumulated and private bureaucratic systems—i.e., business management structures—established themselves. Industrialization began with light export industries (such as textiles) and progressed gradually into the heavy industrial sectors (such as iron) that were needed to supply munitions manufacturers. The forward course of industrialization naturally brought about class struggle. On the one hand, an "efficient" bureaucracy used the police to repress manifestations of this struggle; on the other hand, conflict-avoidance methods such as arbitration and a spirit of national harmony, which stemmed from traditional conformist attitudes, helped alleviate tensions.

Meanwhile, the compulsion to catch up with the West gave rise to unbalanced domestic growth, while abroad it resulted in aggression against neighboring countries that had been "left behind" by progress. Imbalances in domestic development were seen in the differing treatment of cities and villages, since agricultural land was heavily taxed to promote industrialization; as well as between large and small enterprises, where the latter, often subcontractors, were victimized so as to benefit heavy industrial development. In this way a dual structure appeared in the domestic economy and was perpetuated by the constant sacrifices of those sectors in which development lagged, or was not deemed important. In addition, military expenses came to occupy a surprisingly large share of the budget (for example, 47.2 percent of national expenditures in 1931), a situation which led to sacrifices in welfare funds for the people. Forced as they were to consent to so many sacrifices, the people showed a tendency to condone Japan's outward expansion as an outlet for their dissatisfactions. Social Darwinism came to play a predominant role in the attitudes of the time: the victims of domestic progress looked down upon surrounding underdeveloped countries as the "unfit"; that the unfit should fall victims to the strong was justified in the struggle for existence.

Efficient organization of the bureaucracy was accompanied by yet another negative feature of the times: the trampling of human rights under the name of police efficiency. Furthermore, the overwhelming importance of the bureaucracy delayed the development of a representative system of government. Because of the efficient bureaucratic system the goals of the state were executed rationally; but these goals were not decided upon as rationally as was their execution.[5] The fact that more than two out of three prime ministers in this period came from the ranks of civil or military officialdom demonstrates the great weight of bureaucratic influence in Japanese politics. Even after the establishment of party politics, party heads often came from positions in civil or military bureaucracies. Politicians of this type felt only a weak sense of responsibility to the people for the policies they elaborated; they showed a tendency to simply adapt themselves to *faits accomplis*. Thus Tōjō, the prime minister who declared war on the Anglo-American powers, had no consciousness of making this decision himself—he thought of it as a historically inevitable step. In this kind of political system, where no one takes individual responsibility, it is difficult to criticize or to reexamine a state goal once a united popular effort has been started to carry it out. The individual is submerged in a group-oriented society; minority opinions contrary to established group desires are disregarded by a tradition which values group harmony. This process produces a tendency toward national conformism which in turn leads to discrimination against the minority.

Thus, while Japan's modernization was a success insofar as it achieved rapid industrialization, it led domestically to imbalanced development, weak democratic institutions, and repression. Externally, Japan's success propelled it into aggressive war. Until her defeat at the hands of a superior armed force, the Allied powers, Japan proved incapable of controlling these defects from within.

III. The Period since 1945

Value System

Japan's acceptance of the Potsdam Declaration and her Occupation by the Allied forces made it necessary to attempt a change in her basic value system. Demilitarization and democratization were the major policy guidelines. Land reform, the dissolution of the *zaibatsu* (large family combines), the revision of the civil code, and reforms in education and elsewhere, enabled the ideals of the new Constitution of 1947—pacifism, democracy, and respect for fundamental human rights—to take root. The Constitution was drafted by the Occupation authorities, hence these concepts were introduced as a result of outside pressure. But even when Occupation policy changed because of the Cold War, and when Japanese conservatism attempted to amend the Constitution, the Japanese people resisted any tampering with these "imported" concepts. As time has passed, many people have become accustomed to enjoying these freedoms and their rights. In fact the attempted revision in 1958 of the Police Duty Law was thwarted by the people's deep concern over their right of privacy. They now considered the "imported" ideals to be their own, and the Constitution to be one in which they had a vested interest.[6]

Despite the various policies ordered by the Occupation authorities, such as the political purge and the revision of textbooks on Japanese history, and despite the radical changes on the surface resulting from them, both group-orientedness and the goal of catching up with and surpassing the West remained, but with a necessary modification. Postwar group orientation did not center on the state nor on the Emperor; instead it became more directly a form of group belonging— i.e., as an identification with their own family and with their company. Incidentally in Japan "lifetime employment" is the norm, i.e., a worker stays with the same company until his retirement. In fact the disintegration of Imperial ideology did not necessarily mean the emergence of individualism; at least in the first stage, it resulted in competition among various groups with differing goals (such as labor unions, agricultural cooperatives,) released from the monolithic Imperial Rule Assistance Association.

The aim of catching up with and surpassing the West also underwent a metamorphosis, because the option of becoming a great military power was blocked by the Constitution, which made pacifism a national policy. It came to focus primarily on competition with the Western powers in the field of economic development. Instead of conflict by means of warships and other armaments, conflict became competition, centered on the volume of Japan's gross national product and growth rate.

How were the traditional and new elements related to each other in the postwar value system? The rejection of Nazi Germany and the return to the Western liberal democratic model was accelerated by group conformity and the competition among groups. There were some Japanese groups who took as their model the Soviet Union, or later Communist China; but the number was small; later, as the result of the Russian invasions of Hungary and Czechoslovakia and the cultural revolution in China, many people came to reject those countries as models. In the same way, those who thought that the United States ought to be the model for Japan were greatly disillusioned by Vietnam and Watergate.

The popular attitude became more and more realistic and less and less ideological as the economic recovery has continued. The principles of the Constitution have become something in which the Japanese people have a stake, although not many people are aware of them as universal principles. Most people are eager to maintain a peaceful family life; in order to do so they must keep the company for which they are working prosperous. Usually they are not particularly interested in promoting world peace or improving democratic participation, but when they have felt that their peaceful daily life and democratic procedures were in danger, they have protested. Such was the case in 1960 when the Kishi administration used an undemocratic strategy to pass the revised security treaty between the United States and Japan.[7]

To sum up, one of the most important characteristics in the postwar value system is fragmentation. In one sense this means the disappearance of monolithic ultranationalism and the emphasis on a loyalty focused on the immediate group, such as the company or the family—the nuclear family rather than the *ie,* the extended family.[8] In another sense, as the result of privatization in mass society, people's interests are limited to immediate concerns rather than ideological causes.

Organizational Structure

Fragmentation is important in the organizational structure and in value-orientation. The abolition of the Imperial Rule Assistance Association resulted in the fragmentation of its previously unified elements. Immediately after the war more than three hundred political parties (including one-member parties) emerged but the major ones were a revival of prewar parties which had dissolved themselves to join the IRAA. Labor organizations, agricultural organizations, women's and youth's organizations, which had been absorbed by the IRAA, also became independent and re-formed under new "democratic" labels. The organizational structure, however, continued to be the same in the sense that a highly bureaucratized structure on the top was linked with the traditional conformist in-group at the bottom, exemplified by hamlet solidarity in the case of agricultural cooperatives, and workshop solidarity in the case of labor unions. The latter are customarily based upon the enterprise unit. The combination of a bureaucratic structure and a natural sense of solidarity among those living together or working together continued to be the same. However, in its postwar form, it is more characterized by pluralism than was the monolithic structure of prewar organization.

Another difference between pre- and postwar organizational structure is the decline of the importance of ascriptive criteria in the selection of leaders. The dissolution of the *zaibatsu* meant the end of the domination of a few large families in the economic arena; land reform put an end to the hierarchical relationship between landowner and tenants, and the amendment of the civil code brought about the end of the *ie,* the extended family system, and the end of the privileged position of head of the family. The postwar lack of hierarchy facilitated a horizontal solidarity among hamlet members or workplace in-groups.

The new element added in terms of organization was the emergence of voluntary associations. Until the end of World War II, there was no room for voluntary associations in the strict sense, because all groups were subordinate to the emperor system; i.e., in terms of legitimacy all should serve the imperial rule, and in terms of practice be more or less dependent on the government. Only after the defeat in World War II could each organization have its own legitimacy and operate independently of the government. It was, however, another matter whether all organizations really wanted this independence. Organizations such as agricultural cooperatives depended heavily on the government because they collected the rice and received government subsidies. As part of the movement, since the end of the Occupation, toward tighter, government control, Social Education Act was amended in 1959. The amendment now allowed the government to provide the social education groups with government subsidies (a measure prohibited during the occupation to keep those organizations independent of the government). These were attempts on the part of government and the government party, which had been almost permanently in power, to have such organizations secure bloc votes for them. Many economically weaker organizations welcome such attempts to improve the financial condition of the organization and bolster the position of leaders. These leaders usually receive minimal member input because of the traditional organizational structure, mentioned above, in which members' identification with the organization is what is emphasized, without much interest in the actual decision making process.

Only recently have really independent voluntary associations emerged among citizens concerned with pollution or other local issues. The problem of pollution, for instance, has not been solved by political parties or by labor unions. The latter are enterprise-based unions and hence reluctant to tackle the problem because of their fear that the cost of preventing pollution may adversely affect their wages. The citizens felt that they had no organization that could support them and so they started a voluntary organization to tackle this problem. Such organizations often intentionally avoid cooperating with the political parties which may, and in fact often do, manipulate the movement to get bloc votes at election time. These groups are often in confrontation with huge existing organizations, such as political parties, big businesses, and labor unions, but they are still relatively weak in numbers and financially. It is still too early for us to estimate their future importance.

Development

Returning to the original structure in postwar Japan and considering the traditional and new elements both in value orientation and organizational structure, how can the development thereafter be traced? As in the case of the first stage, i.e., after the Restoration of 1868, new elements were more or less related to the Western impact, in this case to the Occupation policy, and hence in the popular Japanese mind, somehow alien. The development which followed can be explained by the relationship between new elements and traditional elements, which were partly in contradition to the former and partly modifying the former so that the new elements could be adjusted to the existing situation. The degree to which the new elements took root is also related to the degree of socioeconomic change resulting from the postwar reforms originally ordered by the Occupation authorities.

Although the principles of the Constitution of 1947 presupposed independent individuals and voluntary associations based upon such individuals, in reality only a few associations emerged with such individualistic commitments; there was no clear distinction between personal commitment and the traditional sense of solidarity. For instance, new agricultural cooperatives were established as voluntary organizations, as distinguished from prewar agricultural organizations whose membership was compulsory. In reality the new cooperatives were in no way different from the prewar models.[9] Very often traditional solidarity overshadowed personal commitment in the long run. Some voluntary associations among intellectuals attempted to be free from any partisan influence, but were later infiltrated by the political parties and either fragmented or disappeared.

The emergence of a great number of groups immediately after defeat in World War II seemed chaotic but very soon a certain regimentation of groups took place. By the time of the emergence of the so-called "two party system" in 1955 as a result of the regrouping of both conservative and socialist forces, the distinction between the "ins" and "outs" became clear. The ideological dichotomization, during the Cold War period made the antagonism between the two camps even more serious. The conservatives called the socialists subversive; the socialists labeled the conservatives "reactionary," "undemocratic," and opposed the spirit of the Constitution.

In fact, the conservative party had the clear intention of amending the Constitution so that Japan could have full-fledged armed forces. Also the conservatives used the arguments that since the Constitution was drafted and handed down by the Occupation authorities, an "independent" Japan ought to revise it. This attempt created not only protest from the opposition camp but also failed to find support among the broader populace. This was because the attempted revision was felt to be a threat to the democratic principles of the Constitution. Fundamental human rights, which were guaranteed for the first time in Japan by the Constitution of 1947, had already become something which the mass of the people held dearly. Having been "given" these rights, Japanese people have strongly resisted any subsequent attempt at curtailment. This sensitivity to any threat to their rights has been increasing, particularly among the younger generation, although this sensitivity does not always flow from a precise awareness of "rights" as distinguished from vested interests.

Similarly, pacifism, another important element of principle in the Constitution, is not always upheld by the Japanese people. However, it is true that most Japanese normally hold pacifist sentiments although the latter are not organized into an articulate set of beliefs. The increased interest of the people in preserving their peaceful existence over a lengthy period tends to produce two paradoxical results: on the one hand, it is the most important obstacle to any attempt to revise the Constitution; on the other, it at once fosters a passive attitude of minimal resistance to the government, even on the matter of defending the Constitution. At any rate, as a result of this popular attitude, the conservative party was forced to give up the idea of revising the Constitution, but the defense budget had continued to grow. Indeed, despite the existence of a constitutional clause forbidding the maintenance of armed forces, Japan's defense spending is ranked eighth in the world.

The government party no longer openly advocates revision of the Constitution in the immediate future and ideological issues have now become less important than economic problems. In particular, after 1960, when a serious protest movement took place concerning the security treaty between the United States and Japan, Prime Minister Ikeda placed greater emphasis on economic growth. Thus the 1960s were characterized by a rapid economic growth in which the public showed great interest.

This increased popular interest in economic prosperity, particularly in consumption, resulted in the general tendency towards privatization in mass society and hence to the increased political apathy. Occasionally, however, if people have a fear that their peaceful daily life is in danger, if they perceive the possibility of being involved in a war, they may become *active* in expressing their interest in maintaining their *peaceful* life. Deep popular concern with the war in Vietnam in the late 1960s showed this clearly.

Economic growth created two problems which are relevant to our theme. In terms of value, very often extremely rapid economic growth threatened human amenities by destroying the environment and even taking or damaging human life, e.g., pollution. Thus the fundamental question, "Regarding development, what should our goal be?" ought to be raised again. In terms of organizational structure, as a result of "free competition" among enterprises, oligopoly emerged. In the late 1950s pressure groups in small and medium sized enterprises were active, but during the rapid economic growth of the 1960s the larger enterprises became yet larger by mergers, by absorbing smaller companies or, by controlling them through subcontracting. As organizations grow in size, increased bureaucratization seems to be an inevitable consequence. Thus huge organizations in various fields, such as in government, big business, and political parties, all interrelated at the very top level, create a strong feeling of alienation in outsiders, and in those in the rank and file of those same organizations.[10] The sense of alienation and irritation, of being powerless, may result in violent resistance, or may more frequently create a sense of resignation. Only a minority may attempt to become independent of such a system by engaging in a voluntary citizens' movement based on personal commitment.

Evaluation

Some things have changed and other things have remained unchanged, but what are the positive and negative aspects of Japan's postwar development?

First, let us look on the bright side. Even if we concede that pacifism, democracy, and respect for human rights are not yet strong enough to orient and direct Japanese politics, we can at least expect that they possess enough strength to hold back any threat to the principles of the Constitution. Examples would include the opposition to nuclear arms, opposition to the Kishi cabinet's undemocratic way of passing the revised U.S.-Japan Security Treaty in 1960, and the opposition to enterprises which disregard the human rights of pollution victims.

Next, because pacifism has made full-fledged rearmament impossible, there are no heavy military financial burdens on the economy. Thus Japanese industries have been able to develop by responding to growth in domestic demand. The dissolution of the *zaibatsu* and the land reform have corrected imbalances in domestic development; higher wages for workers, a result of the postwar union movement, have brought about an expansion of domestic demand that has also been desirable from a business point of view. Strong identification with one's company, efficient management, free competition—these have been contributing factors to rapid postwar economic growth.

On the other hand, there have also been negative aspects in this rapid postwar development. A variety of inequalities and injustices were created as a result of the belief that everyone should be able to compete equally, since family background now no longer played the role it once had. Oligopoly developed as strong companies swallowed up weaker companies through mergers and brought subcontracting enterprises under their control. Moreover, so as not to weaken the country's international economic competitiveness, administrative guidance by the bureaucracy and legislature has weakened the antitrust system, thus increasing this tendency toward oligopoly. Large enterprises have strengthened their political influence by contributing to political campaigns but have not given sufficient consideration to the victims of pollution. These actions have provided the impetus for strong opposition movements. The unions, too, the majority of which are organized within large enterprises, eager in their pursuit of wage demands and caught in the framework of the enterprise labor union, all too often lack empathy for pollution victims and the small subcontractors exploited by the large corporations. Furthermore, the close identification of company employees with their company has led to a tendency to think that one is always working for the benefit of the company by adopting any means, including bribery to that end. This method of operation is linked to political corruption, a fact that can be seen in the largescale bribes that accompanied the purchase of aircraft in the recent Lockheed case. Vulgarized Social Darwinism and a belief in the survival of the fittest have justified the acts of the strong and created a situation in which the victims of rapid economic growth are perceived as weak. Not only has this led to discrimination against the weak in Japan, it has also invited condescension toward those countries that seem to have been left behind. For example, it has led to the ridiculing of the "English Disease." Moreover, in its economic advance into Southeast Asia, Japan, secure in the conviction of Japanese economic superiority, has tended to ignore the negative aspects of its penetration.

Unlike the prewar period, in today's Japan there is considerable freedom of opinion. The Japanese themselves have criticized the negative points I have discussed here and there are a good number of movements underway to correct them. However, the economically strong have grown surprisingly stronger, and large bureaucratic organizations (including the existing political parties) overwhelmingly dominate the political world and nearly all other areas of Japanese society. As might be expected, small-scale spontaneous citizens' movements which seek to correct these defects have not reached the point where they can bring about satisfactory reforms.

Notes

1. The traditional way of avoiding conflict by enlarging the in-group unit to absorb the conflicting parties is analyzed in detail in Takeshi Ishida, "Conflict and Conflict Accomodation in Japan: Viewed in Terms of *Omote-Ura* and *Uchi-Soto* Relations," E. Krauss et al. (eds.), *Conflict in Japan* (forthcoming).
2. For more details concerning the impact of urbanization, see Takeshi Ishida, "Urbanization and Its Impact on Japanese Politics—the Case of a

Late and Rapidly Developed Country," *Annals of the Institute of Social Science,* University of Tokyo, no. 8, March 1967.

3. The train fare for unemployed urban workers returning to their native villages was paid by the government as a social relief measure. See R. P. Dore, *Land Reform in Japan,* London, Oxford University Press, 1959, p. 88.

4. *Sangyō Hōkokukai* was formally established in 1940, but starting from 1937 police and other bureaucrats in the Home Ministry encouraged the formation of organizations composed of both management and labor to avoid labor disputes. The establishment of *Sampō* indicated the final institutionalization of such efforts.

5. One of the features of modernization in Japan was that greater emphasis was placed on the process of goal-achievement rather than the process of goal-establishment. In this regard, see Takeshi Ishida, "Development of Interest Groups and the Pattern of Political Modernization in Japan," Robert E. Ward (ed.), *Political Development in Modern Japan,* Princeton University Press, 1968, pp. 293–336.

6. For details, see Takeshi Ishida, "Emerging or Eclipsing Citizenship?—A Study of Changes in Political Attitudes in Postwar Japan," *The Developing Economies,* vol. 6, no. 4, Dec. 1968.

7. For details concerning the security treaty crisis of 1960, see George R. Packard III, *Protest in Tokyo: the Security Treaty Crisis of 1960,* Princeton University Press, 1966.

8. *Ie* literally means house but has a special connotation. The *ie* was characterized by the following features: (1) It was an extended family (that is, a main family and its branches) and there existed a hierarchical relationship among the main and branch families. (2) Each family within the *ie* was patriarchal in structure. (3) Members of the family owed obedience to the head of the family, and the branch families owed allegiance to the main family. In return, the main family provided a kind of "social security" for the branch families in time of need, and the head of each family provided similar security for the members of his family. (4) The solidarity of the *ie,* and filial piety, institutionalized in the hierarchical structure of the *ie,* were the ideological basis for the family-state idea. For more details, see Takeshi Ishida, *Japanese Society,* New York, Random House, 1971, p. 49f.

9. For details concerning agricultural cooperatives, see Aurelia D. George and Takeshi Ishida, " 'Nokyo': The Japanese Farmers' Representative," Peter Drysdale et al. (eds.), *Japan and Australia: Two Societies and their Interaction,* Australian National University Press, 1981.

10. The interrelationship between bureaucracy, big business and the ruling government party (LDP) was discussed in detail in Takeshi Ishida, "Interest Groups under a Semipermanent Government Party: the Case of Japan," *The Annals of the American Academy of Political and Social Science,* May 1974.

CHAPTER TWO

The Integration of Conformity and Competition

I. Introduction

Any analytical framework which seeks to explain Japan's modern value system must encompass both the positive and the negative aspects of Japan's modernization experience. It is my contention that the integration of conformity and competition offers such a framework.

Every society contains, to a varying degree, elements of conformity and of competition. What is unique about Japan is that these two elements are so closely intertwined within its social and cultural context. If we follow R. K. Merton's definition of conformity as a mode of adaptation which accepts the cultural goals and institutional means of a given society, conformity can only be understood statically—and not as a dynamic process.[1] But in Japan, conformity, by integration with competition, is able to respond to changes and thereby to assume a dynamic nature. As I shall show later, once a group demands a new attitude from its members, competitive loyalty within a conformity-oriented group—that is, competition in order to contribute to the maintenance and growth of the group—brings abrupt changes to the group. Two such instances come immediately to mind: (1) In the second half of the nineteenth century when Japan abandoned her seclusion policy in favor of Westernization and adopted a policy of industrialization in order to realize the goal of "rich nation and strong military," and (2) after defeat in World War II, when Japan abandoned her xenophobic attitude and devoted all her energies to carrying out a series of social reforms under the auspices of the Occupation authorities.

Competition, when integrated with the conformity prevalent in a closed group, can alleviate rather than exacerbate intragroup conflicts

23

which threaten the very existence of the group. As is well known, groups of all kinds in Japan, beset with factionalism, avoid fatal schisms by commanding a high degree of conformity when threatened from outside. Even disputes between labor and management, supposedly based on irreconcilable ideological differences, are often in fact fought only over principles and not over anything concrete. The reason why demands for wage increases are seldom unreasonable is that competition and dispute are always between companies and their unions, which for all practical purposes belong to the same conformity-oriented group, which is competing with other domestic or foreign enterprises. Therefore, the integration between conformity and competition performs a very useful function in Japanese society.

Yet we cannot ignore the negative aspects of this integration. Its greatest weakness is that competition for loyalty within a closed conformity-oriented group gives rise to "a system of irresponsibility."[2] Before World War II, orthodoxy in Japan contained no systematic doctrine. Rather, it was based solely on the belief that the emperor had always reigned, and "thus" should continue to reign, over Japan throughout its history. Under such conditions—where even constitutionalism was used merely as a tool to facilitate Imperial rule—competition in loyalty embodied elements whose consequences were totally unpredictable. Once competition in loyalty began, it became impossible to control and impossible to resist. Political leaders may have used "competition in loyalty" for their own ends but once ultranationalism gripped the country and patriotism, "the last refuge of scoundrels," became a pliable tool for extremists of every political hue, the political leaders lost control.[3] Furthermore, buttressed by the tradition of identifying the natural order with the social order, people looked upon the upsurge of ultranationalism as a natural phenomenon something akin to a typhoon.[4] There is also the question of the responsibility of the emperor, whom the Japanese people regarded as the focus of their absolute loyalty. As the tide of the war turned against Japan, all that the emperor could do was to remark in private to the minister of foreign affairs, "It would be nice if the war stopped soon."[5] In a system like this, it is hardly surprising that responsible decision makers were nowhere to be found.

The origin of the elements of conformity and competition dates back to early Japanese history, but their integration did not become a regular feature of Japanese society until modern times. Moreover, depending on which particular period in Japan's modern history is being discussed, the two elements were integrated quite differently.

The approach adopted here will be as follows. I shall describe the historic changes which have occurred in both conformity and competition. For the sake of convenience, these will be explained separately. Then, against this historical background, I shall explain the elements which have brought about their integration. I shall pay particular attention to the lack of the transcendental element in Japan's religious tradition. In particular, the popular belief in biocosmic energy will be offered as an important contributing factor for the integration of conformity and competition. Finally, I will analyse the particular mode of integration prevalent in contemporary Japan and the problem it has created and may create in the future.

II. Conformity in a closed "In-group"

Most Japanese scholars find that the traditional rural community provides the prototype of conformity which characterizes Japanese society. Since the Japanese people from early times settled and grew rice on what little land they had, it is hardly surprising that conformity became a dominant characteristic of Japan's rural communities. Furthermore, since rural communities formed along rivers or in delta regions were self-sufficient and relatively isolated from each other by mountain ranges, it was natural that they should have developed into tightly closed in-groups.[6] It is not surprising therefore that, during the course of many centuries, the rule of conformity came to dominate village life, and failure to conform was punishable by ostracism. Since village families lived in the same region for centuries, there gradually developed among them, through intermarriage, relationships of stem and branch families as well as networks of affinal ties. These blood ties helped strengthen village solidarity considerably.

Under the partly centralized feudalistic system of the Tokugawa period from the beginning of the seventeenth century, villagers were required to remain permanently in their villages and to pay taxes to the *han* (fief) government, which had the effect of institutionalizing the closed in-group common to rural communities. While the villagers could maintain ties with the *han* through the payment of taxes, and the *han* could in turn maintain ties with the shogunate in Edo (Tokyo) through the institution of *sankinkotai* (alternate-year residence in Edo), there were no means by which individual villages could relate to each other horizontally and attenuate their isolation.

When the Meiji Restoration leaders took measures to establish a centralized state, the villages were incorporated as subunits within the prefectures that replaced the old *han* as the administrative divisions of the central government. (The prefectures were placed under the authority of governors appointed by the central government.) Although people were allowed the right to freely choose their occupations and residences, very few left their villages. The Meiji oligarchy, however, strictly limited the association of people from different villages in order to prevent people's rights movements from extending beyond the confines of a single village. On the other hand, the oligarchy attempted to utilize the villages' strong sense of conformity as a means of promoting conformity on a national scale.

The solidarity, partly based upon blood ties, which had contributed to the formation of conformity in rural communities, was expanded to encompass the whole nation. The family-state idea which considered the imperial family as the main family in the nation and thus treated the relationship between the emperor and his subjects as a form of family relationship, played an important role in strengthening national conformity.

Of course, the fear that Japan's independence was being endangered by harsh developments in the world at large was one of the important factors that contributed to the strengthening of conformity in the newborn nation-state. Yet another important factor was Japan's so-called homogeneity. There are many conflicting theories concerning the origin of the Japanese people, and no convincing solution seems likely because their ancestors arrived in the Japanese islands very early in man's history. Because the sporadic immigrations from the Korean peninsula ceased after the ninth century, and because a single race of people lived for the next ten centuries on this group of islands in almost complete geographic isolation, there soon developed among the people similarities of language, customs, and values that served as foundations for the development of the new nation-state. One reason why the Meiji government was able to abandon its policy of "expulsion of the foreigners" and quickly adopt a policy of Westernization—ranging from Western legal systems to Western life styles—was that the people shared a very strong sense of being Japanese.

As an important part of its Westernization program, the Meiji government extended the conformity found in the isolated villages to the prefectural and finally to the national level. In this way, the concentric sphere of influence of the closed in-group at the village level was extended to the prefectural and ultimately to the national level. Disputes that persisted between villages—such as those involving irrigation rights—and between prefectures vying to procure as much funding from the central government as possible, were managed by expanding the size of the in-group and incorporating the parties involved into the expanded in-group.

Needless to say, the actual disputes were not eliminated by conceptually defining the national state as an in-group with a high degree of conformity. The peasants, in particular, were opposed to the government's rapid industrialization program since they had to bear the burden of financing it by paying the exorbitant taxes that the government levied on their land. In the Meiji period, the farming class constituted by far the largest group in the voting population. Thus the majority of Diet members were from the rural areas. Therefore, the early Diet sessions were characterized by disputes which inevitably ensued between rural representatives demanding reduction of land taxes and a government trying to promote its industrialization program. However, the Sino-Japanese War (1894–95) and the Russo-Japanese War (1904–05) served to heighten the conformity of the entire nation and to distract the disputing parties from engaging in further confrontation.

However, modern social differentiation was an inevitable result of Japan's rapid industrial development after World War I. The deepening differences between landowners and tenants, and between labor and capital, became apparent in the 1920s, when clashes between these elements began to increase. The 1930s was a period in which policies were implemented to revive conformity on the national level in order to cope with these clashes. When the Great Depression of 1929 hit Japan and devastated the country, particularly the rural communities, efforts were immediately made to restore order in the villages. Large landowners and absentee landlords were restrained from making excessive profits, while those independent farmers and landlords who cultivated their own land were placed at the center of village life where they could take an active part in cooperatives and help to restore conformity to the rural communities.

The government also adopted policies aimed at mitigating the increasing number of disputes between management and labor which were affecting the urban centers. Members of the urban working class, mostly second and third sons of farming families, maintained ties with their native villages as a place they could return to in case they lost their jobs or retired. As industrialization progressed, however, they came to feel more and more estranged from their villages, which ironically heightened their nostalgia for the traditional village life. It was not difficult for the government to take advantage of such a situation and transform the relationship just as it has similarly transformed the relationship between landowners and tenant farmers. The government thus created an ideology of family enterprise—employer and employees as members of the same company "family"—that served to mitigate the conflict between labor and management. In this way, the state, as the main family, incorporated the enterprise into its household as smaller branch families.

Kokumin Seishin Sōdōin Undō (The National Spirit Mobilization Movement) was put into effect in the latter half of the 1930s to integrate the rural and urban reorganization programs. In considering the rise of patriotic national conformity which this movement reflected, it is necessary to bear two important factors in mind: (1) the spread of universal education, particularly compulsory primary education, and (2) the increasing influence of the mass media crucial to the emergence of a mass society. Primary education became compulsory in 1872. By the end of the nineteenth century, 90 percent of boys and 80 percent of girls were attending school; and by the end of the 1920s nearly 100 percent of both sexes were enrolled in school. At the primary level, in addition to the usual three R's, the Imperial Rescript on Education of 1890 introduced moral education into the school curriculum as a means of promoting patriotism. The standardization brought about by a universal education strengthened national conformity. In addition the peculiarly Japanese input, i.e., moral education, helped prevent disputes in villages and factories by instilling in the people the virtue of "harmony."

Incidentally, the conscription system introduced in 1873 was another method by which male subjects not only received training in discipline and morals but also underwent a standardized educational experience which prepared them for an active role in Japan's modernizing process.

The spread of education and the rising rate of literacy considerably aided the development of the mass media. Even as early as the beginning of this century, the three national newspapers boasted a circulation of more than 100,000 apiece, and by 1920 their circulations had each surpassed the one million mark. Moreover, accompanying the increase in circulation, in order to secure as wide and varied a readership as possible, the newspapers began to appeal more and more to the monolithic nature of national conformity by assuming the role of a transmitter of news rather than a carrier of specific points of view. Nor were the newspapers alone. Popular magazines such as *King,* a monthly that nearly doubled its circulation from 740,000 in 1925 (the year it was founded) to 1.4 million in 1933, served a vital role in fostering national conformity among the masses.

The Japanese invasion of Manchuria in 1931, the subsequent withdrawal from the League of Nations and the Washington Treaty System, the invasion of the Chinese mainland, and the increasing international tension combined to further strengthen national conformity. This phenomenon conformed to the general sociological principle that an in-group strengthens its internal cohesion when it is in dispute with an external group.

What effect did Japan's defeat in World War II, and the resultant shattering of monolithic national integration, have on national conformity? Under the Occupation, all extreme nationalist groups were broken up, ultranationalists were purged, and nationalistic education was abolished. The army and the navy were banned, and a new "peace Constitution" was promulgated containing the famous Article 9 renouncing war forever. The Constitution embraced democratic principles and guaranteed fundamental human rights. Finally, with the dissolution of the Home Ministry, the centralized police state effectively came to an end.

Yet these measures did not signal a complete breakdown of national conformity. In addition to ideological disputes between political parties, the appearance of labor unions and farmer unions provided an additional impetus for the labor movement. Indeed it looked, at one time, as if the pro-Establishment conservative party and the opposition forces supported by the labor-farmer movement were on a collision course. However, the labor-farmer movements, which had called for a socialist revolution, gradually declined in influence after a general strike scheduled for February 1, 1947 was suppressed by the Occupation authorities. It should also be pointed out that the land reform and the growth of agricultural cooperatives combined to weaken the peasant movement's *raisons d'être*. This was particularly true after the economic recovery of the 1950's, when the workers began to focus their interests on increasing their share of the cake by enlarging the size of the cake itself through economic growth. In the labor field, it goes without saying that the institutions of lifetime employment and enterprise unions, both unique to Japan, helped to strengthen the workers' sense of identity with their company.

In postwar Japan, of course, there is neither a clearly defined national goal around which national conformity can be focused nor is the central government's control strong enough to create such conformity. The relatively extensive recognition of freedom of speech permits various viewpoints to exist, and since the monolithic Imperial Rule Assistance Association was disbanded after the war, there naturally emerged a variety of interest groups all able to engage in free competition. On the other hand, because Japan had to relinquish her colonies at the end of World War II, its linguistic, cultural, and racial homogeneity is today even more pronounced than it was during the war. Despite the absence of government pressure, the three leading national papers (each with a circulation in the millions), along with radio and television, now transmit remarkably uniform information, so that a real sense of conformity still persists in the popular mind. This dormant conformity suddenly flowers when Japan hosts international events, such as the 1964 Tokyo Olympics and the 1970 Osaka World Exposition.

The rapid economic growth of the 1960s and the accompanying emergence of Japan as an economic superpower have served to increase popular confidence. In my conclusions, I shall consider whether this tendency will result in the reappearance of a more extreme form of nationalism in Japan.

III. The Dynamism of Competition

An excellent historical example of the competitive attitude in Japan can be seen in the behavior of the independent warriors who rampaged the land during the Warring States period from the thirteenth to the sixteenth centuries. In times of incessant turbulence, a free warrior could expand his sphere of influence and improve his status by defeating his rivals in military contests. A fight to the death was thought to offer the best opportunity for success and prosperity.

The advent of the Tokugawa shogunate in the beginning of the 17th century, and the subsequent 300 years of relative peace, in theory removed all reason for military rivalries. The military arts were ritualized into a kind of athletic exercise, while the warriors became patrimonial bureaucrats serving the *han* governments. Their status became hereditary, and competition for upward mobility became a thing of the past. As long as they were patrimonial bureaucrats influenced by Chinese tradition, it was natural that Confucianism, which was the dominant philosophy of the Chinese bureaucrats, became their orthodoxy. But the Tokugawa bureaucrats, as warriors, were pragmatic and placed great importance on the ability to adapt to any contingencies. Particularly in the critical period at the close of the Tokugawa shogunate, despite their low hereditary ranking as warriors, those who possessed practical skills and the ability to deal with international crisis became increasingly influential. Thus the social conditions at the close of the Tokugawa shogunate set the stage for a new form of competition which exhibited features very much like those found in the chaotic Warring States period.

The Meiji Restoration, which was strongly influenced by the lower ranking samurai, abolished, in principle, the feudalistic distinctions in social status and promoted free and unbiased competition between individuals. For example, Samuel Smiles' *Self Help* was translated into Japanese in 1870 and attained remarkable popularity. Social Darwinism, which began to spread rapidly in Japan from the 1880s, became the theoretical basis for the social significance of competition. What happened to competition in Japan? The Meiji Restoration's elimination of feudalistic status distinctions combined with the spread of universal education and the adoption of a form of meritocracy (strictly speaking, a system of employment based on educational background and performance on a qualifying examination, with promotion based on competition among individuals with the same number of years of seniority) inspired every man of every class to aspire to "one day become a state minister or a general." As is the case with most societies, the idea of equality that the Meiji Restoration championed was nothing but a myth. Nevertheless, even though only the well-educated and the relatively wealthy were actually able to succeed, granted some outstanding exceptions, the myth was attractive enough to inspire the masses to enthusiastic participation in the competition for success.

But in Japan, where national conformity was strongly emphasized, it was not feasible to carry this principle of competition too far. Unrestrained competition would have disrupted domestic harmony. In a conformity-conscious society like Japan, competition takes the form of competition to prove one's loyalty, whether to the emperor or to the state, and thus embodies accommodation to the prevailing social order. In other words, the person who actually succeeds and enjoys both wealth and prestige is seen to deserve what he has because he has contributed more to the state. But on the other hand, those who are unsuccessful are condemned on two counts: not only are they condemned as failures, they also stand accused of not having been sufficiently loyal to the state.

Yet even those who are condemned to failure could theoretically discount their plight by claiming that they were actually more loyal to the state than were the successful. While it is true that competition in loyalty makes it possible to reconcile the principle of competition's inherent conflict with conformity and to make competition a vital feature of the conformity-oriented national group, it is also true that such a process incurs new difficulties such as determining how to (and who will) measure accurately any particular individual's degree of loyalty.

Under imperial rule, the orthodoxy could claim legitimacy only from the belief that Japan had always been ruled by emperors ever since the dawning of her history. Thus in the imperial state, there was no standard against which to measure an individual's loyalty except that of whether or not that individual acted in accordance with the emperor's will. But the emperor in principle never and in practice very rarely expressed his personal opinion. Instead, it was generally believed that the will of the emperor was reflected in the politicies which the cabinet drafted on the advice of elder statesmen and which the bureaucratic machinery implemented after their adoption by the Diet. But there were many who were dissatisfied with such policies, and they had every reason to doubt the authenticity of the claim that cabinet policies were the manifestation of the emperor's will and to suspect that the policies actually reflected the interests of the rich and the powerful. It was doubts such as these that led the group of young officers to assassinate a number of prominent elder statesmen in an attempted military coup on February 26, 1936, for the assassins believed that the true will of the emperor—which they, as right-wing radicals, considered beneficial to the country—could be realized only if the "wicked elements" were eliminated.

Herein lay the pitfall inherent in the competition in loyalty of a conformity-oriented society. Although it was possible to forcibly suppress such acts of violence against the state, it was more difficult to refute the radical officers' logic. In fact, although the bulk of the dissatisfied ordinary citizens were opposed to what the radical right did, many were sympathetic to or even in accord with their cause. Thus while the military coup could be suppressed, no principles existed which could halt the rightward drift in public opinion. From the premise that even constitutionalism had been granted by imperial favor, constitutionalism could logically have only secondary significance, leaving the Diet and the political parties vulnerable to attacks from the right. The mood of the radical right overshadowed the logic of political realism, and fanaticism prevailed over reason. The rise of ultranationalism went unchecked until Japan's defeat in World War II. What caused the great tragedy was competition in loyalty and institutionalized irresponsibility.

The war leveled practically every city in Japan; agricultural land reform took the land from the landlord; the political purge stripped former leaders of their status; and the dissolution of the zaibatsu put an end to the economic dominance of a few tremendously wealthy families. It was under these conditions that the Japanese people, under more egalitarian conditions, once again started competing with each other. Moreover, the emperor was no longer a god and his word no longer absolute. This meant that it was no longer necessary to restrict competition to demonstrations of loyalty to the emperor. Competition gained complete legitimacy under new guidelines based on the principles of democracy.

The immediate postwar years also saw the flowering of a popular form of Social Darwinism. Before the war, social welfare—although it amounted to nothing more than charity—was sustained by the idea that the emperor's subjects, "his children," were equal before the emperor and that every subject had to be protected.

It was difficult for the democratic principle of inalienable rights to take root in Japan because, unlike the West, Japan had no religious tradition contending that all men are equal in the eyes of God. The vulgarization of the principle of survival of the fittest is reflected in the unguarded remark in January 1972 by a minister of labor, K. Hara, that if old people had to live in public homes for the elderly, it was their own fault.

An oligopoly developed as a result of the competition carried out under the postwar myth of equality. Up to the second half of the 1950s, there were many economic interest groups competing for political influence, but during the economic growth of the 1960s, many large companies merged and became even bigger, while the small and medium-sized companies became subcontractors or entered into other forms of subordination with these giant firms. The social distinctions between strong and weak thus became fixed, and the question as to who would win the competition between them became a foregone conclusion.

The decision to ease the antitrust regulations—on the grounds that monopoly was needed to make Japanese goods more competitive in international markets and thus to increase Japan's GNP—further widened the gap between strong and weak. The monolithic national integration of the pre-war period disappeared after the war, and no effort was made to explicitly establish international competition as a national goal. The path to becoming a military power was blocked by the "peace Constitution." However, the strategy of achieving economic growth by competing with the industrialized countries of the West did achieve a tacit national consensus. Of course, we cannot overlook the role played by the business-oriented Ministry of International Trade and Industry (MITI) and other ministries in weakening antitrust laws and strengthening the international competitiveness of Japanese goods. Nonetheless, this tacit national consensus had the effect of restricting competition within Japan. In this sense, the pre-war integration of the principle of national conformity and the principle of national competition continues to exist even today, albeit in slightly altered form.

Although the competition in loyalty under the prewar imperial system no longer exists, the substitute belief in the supremacy of economic growth appears to have spread in its place, supported by a tacit national consensus, unhindered by any principle that might constitute an obstacle. Just as those who did not succeed in life under the imperial system were automatically condemned as less loyal to the state, those who do not succeed under the system of rapid economic growth are condemned as lazy or incompetent and therefore possibly disloyal. By international extension, Japan justified her economic expansion into the Third World by arguing that the people of these regions were too lazy to achieve economic development by themselves. Recently, the belief in the primacy of economic growth has even given rise to an attitude, epitomized in such epithets as "the English disease" of condescension toward those Western countries which Japan has surpassed in terms of economic growth.

The principle of competition within a conformist pursuit of economic growth not only results in the various contradictions which excess competition normally creates, but provides a pretext for discriminating against the unsuccessful by stripping them of their legitimate claim to full citizenship. The most extreme instance is the treatment of pollution victims, who cannot afford to move from the polluted area. People whose health was damaged by cadmium and organic mercury waste from factories have often concealed their affliction for fear that public disclosure would jeopardize their own or their relatives' chances for marriage and employment.[7]

The Japanese have finally begun to reflect on these conditions, partly in order to conform to the international standard of an economic superpower. They have begun to question the meaning of economic growth and to doubt whether the policy of placing absolute priority on GNP makes people really happy. The impact of this reflection on Japan's future will be discussed in the last section of this chapter. Before that, let us take a second look at the historical background of the integration of conformity and competition in Japanese society.

IV. Factors Integrating Conformity and Competition

In order to explain how it was possible for conformity, a static concept, and competition, a dynamic concept, to become integrated in Japanese society, it is necessary to examine the religious consciousness existing in the traditional Japanese mentality. If the term religious consciousness is taken to mean consciousness of an absolute and transcendental god, then it must be concluded that religious consciousness does not exist in Japanese tradition. Yet as used here, religious consciousness is taken in the wider sense of belief in the existence of some form of transcendent or eternal being.

It is important here to note the fact that Japanese mythology concerns itself not with the creation of heaven and earth, but with their brith, or more accurately, with the birth of the state. The first point here is that this is dealt with in Japanese mythology not as an act of creation but as a natural formation. In other words, to borrow M. Eliade's terminology, Japanese mythology contains a biocosmic perspective.[8]. The second point is that this was tied to the mundane political community from the beginning. In other words, Japanese mythology considers the universe as a naturally formed organic entity including the mundane political community and inherently containing the biocosmic energy to enable it to develop of its own accord.

The concept of organic formation considers the state as being an organic order of inherent conformity. The state, organically integrated and with one uniform will, is considered oblivious to the decision-making process of the state's organs, and it is believed that the effective realization of the state's presumed uniformity of will is the manifestation of its inherent energy. Therefore, it is believed that competition in an organically integrated state must not be allowed to disrupt the organic order of the state; and that expansion beyond its boundaries is the natural expression of the state's inherent energy. Hiroyuki Katō's espousal of the organic theory of the state domestically and competition for survival internationally was particularly suited to this traditional mentality.

At the time of the Russo-Japanese War, Ruikō Kuroiwa, one of the most popular writers of the day, wrote a piece entitled *Yo ga shinzuru Enerugizumu (My Belief in Energyism)* in which he expounded the idea that war is unavoidable as a natural expression of energy which "once activated, stays activated for ever." In a notorious pamphlet, *Kokubō no Hongi to Sono Kyōka no Teishō (Fundamental Principles of National Defense and Proposals for its Reinforcement, 1934)*, the War Ministry contended that "since 'national defense' is a fundamental part of the vitality which goes into the formation and development of the state, war is the father of creativity and the mother of culture. For individuals going through the ordeal of war, as well as for nations competing with other nations, war is both the motive and the incentive for the formation and development of life and for the creation of culture." Although such outrageous remarks were, at first, heard only from the military, three years later, the Ministry of Education's *Kokutai no Hongi (Essence of the National Polity, 1937)* designed to demonstrate the legitimacy of the ideology of the imperial system went so far as to insist that the invasion of Manchuria was "the unavoidable expression of the national vitality."

This view which considers social phenomena as natural events affirms all that has happened as a result of some natural process. Not only that, it calls for more vigorous manifestation of the national energy, and thus for the adoption of a program of international expansion as a means of ensuring the nation's future—regardless of the soundness of the adventure or its logical outcome. The fact that this sort of thinking influenced public opinion is one reason why, in the rivalry among the various political forces, the policy of international cooperation advocated by elder statesmen and party politicians supposedly in positions closest to the center of power, had to yield before the uncompromising expansionist policy of the right-wing extremists. Furthermore, once competition in loyalty produced ultranationalism, there was nothing that could stop an accompanying outburst of natural energy.

It has been noted above that nothing could be done to curb this endless competition of loyalty because Japanese orthodoxy lacked principles, yet it is also possible to explain this as the Japanese religious consciousness not including transcendental factors derived from an absolute. However, this is not to imply that the Japanese religious consciousness was completely devoid of transcendental factors. Although Buddhism, which arrived in Japan in the sixth century, was not monotheistic, it did contain a belief in the existence of a transcendental, otherworldly being. In the thirteenth century, Buddhism actually went through a period of transcendental revival akin to what Max Weber referred to as a religious reformation.[9] However, from its first adoption by the Japanese ruling class, Buddhism as a whole tended to coalesce with the worldly order through its practice of "interdependence of worldly rule and Buddhist rule." Even after the thirteenth century "reformation," the Tokugawa shogunate later instituted a system requiring every resident to register on the rolls of one of the local Buddhist temples in order to facilitate the ban on Christianity. This system greatly enhanced the temple's function as an administrative organ at the grassroots level and further accelerated Buddhism's coalescence with the worldly order.

It is characteristic of Japanese religion, be it Japanized Buddhism or Shintoism, that the transcendental element always comes to play an important role in connection with some mundane means. For example, the belief in the immortality of the state gave rise to self-sacrificing devotion to the state. Such a concept not only tended to deify the state but served as a basis upon which to criticize aspects of state rule by reference to the eternal history of the state. This is what happened when the radical right tried to overthrow the government. Similarly, respect for "the family name" (the honor of the *ie*) combined with ancestral worship to produce the idea that an individual should not be concerned with his immediate welfare but should believe in the immortality of the *ie* and willingly sacrifice himself for its honor.

Until Japan's defeat in World War II, people believed that the emperor was divine, but only in the sense that he symbolized the immortality of the state. The idea of a personal charisma attached to an individual emperor, such as the Emperor Meiji, was the exception rather than the rule in the modern era. The term that should be used is Max Weber's "hereditary charisma."[10] Thus even though the emperor personally denied his divinity after the war, such a mere personal disclaimer cannot mark a decisive break with the past so long as the 1947 constitutional provision that defines the emperor as "the symbol of the state and of the unity of the people" remains in force. More important was the ebbing of belief in the concept of the eternal state when the Occupation authorities ordered the separation of state and Shintoism, a halt to the teaching of mythology-ridden history, and a cessation of patriotism-exalting moral education. It can even be said that belief in the state's immortality has disappeared among the younger generation, as reflected in their increasing sensitivity to their individual interests and rights.

Yet while belief in the immortality of the state has disappeared, people continue even today to acknowledge the immortality of secular groups closer to them and frequently to sacrifice themselves for the sake of these groups. In February 1979, an executive of a large company killed himself. Since he was the top sales executive for the company involved in a scandal over aircraft imports from America (Lockheed incident) he was one of the few people in a position to know all the secrets concerning the scandal. Yet he committed suicide and took these secrets to the grave forever. According to the newspapers, he left a suicide note in which he wrote, "The company is eternal. It is our duty to devote our lives to that eternity. Our employment may last for only 20 or 30 years, but the life of the company is eternal. I must be brave and act as a man to protect that eternal life."

Of course, most of today's young people would reject the idea of sacrificing themselves for any cause of group. They would undoubtedly reject the ideas expressed in that suicide note. Nevertheless, I wonder if they will feel the same way when they have worked for the same company for 20 years and serve as company executives. I say this for two reasons: (1) Although the commitment to private interests is becoming stronger, private interests in Japan do not mean the interests of the individual but rather mean the interests of the family—although the family no longer denotes the *ie* but rather signifies the nuclear family. (2) In Japan, with its widespread system of lifetime employment, the family's interests still tend to be identified with the company's interests.

From the foregoing, it is clear that the Japanese belief in a transcendental entity is not a belief in an absolute; instead it is rather in one form or another closely tied to human groups, and hence on the same dimension as attitudes toward human groups. The original Shinto festivals were often related to the productive process of the community, events in which the community members ate, drank, and celebrated with the gods. There were no insurmountable barriers separating gods and men. Instead, familiarity and continuity existed between them. The fact that people worshipped the dead as gods confirms this relationship. Although many local communities have revived their traditional festivals, this should not be interpreted as a religious festival, for people attend these festivals not so much out of religious belief but rather as a form of recreation. Nevertheless, there is one public opinion survey which suggests that Buddhism and Shintoism are currently undergoing a revival of sorts. While the number of people who believed in Shintoism and/or Buddhism gradually declined between 1950 and 1973, the number actually increased in the following five years.[11]

However, it is important to bear in mind that this renewed interest in religion most often relates to mundane interests—frequently those of the nuclear family. If there is someone preparing for an entrance examination, that person or some other member of the family may go to a shrine to buy a talisman which they believe will help the student pass examinations; people may go to Buddhist temples to buy safety amulets to ward off traffic accidents; or whole families may visit a shrine or temple during the New Year holidays to pray for prosperity in the coming year. Many Japanese offer prayers both in Buddhist temples and at Shinto shrines without any sense of inconsistency. Indeed, most Japanese get married according to the Shinto rites and buried according to the Buddhist rites. Few people look upon either of these as religious events. In most cases, people have Shinto weddings and Buddhist funerals simply because it is convenient to defer to custom as arranged by the service companies which usually take care of these things.

There was one case in which a group of citizens filed a lawsuit against the city for allegedly violating the constitutional principle of the separation of religion and state when the city held the standard Shinto groundbreaking ceremony asking the gods to protect the workers against accidents. The court held that the ceremony was simply a custom and of no religious significance. There are many ritualized religious functions tied to worldly interests, but their religious significance is not at all clear.

The religious sentiment of the Japanese was so closely tied up with the mundane interests of worldly groups that at times it was impossible to draw the line between the sacred and the secular. This close relationship between the two domains facilitated the individual's contribution to the group and thus contributed to Japan's modernization. This is why Japan's rapid and thorough modernization was not accompanied by an equally rapid and thorough secularization.

In the foregoing, we have examined the historical development of conformity and competition and the factors that caused the two to become integrated. In the last section, we shall conclude with a look at the contemporary situation that has resulted from this integration and touch briefly upon the outlook for the future.

V. The Problems of Contemporary Japanese Society and Its Future

Today conformity dominates in every advanced industrialized society. Erich Fromm refers to this as the dominance of "anonymous authority."[12] In the sense that "anonymous authority" also dominates in Japan, Japan is no different from other advanced industrialized nations. Most students of modern Japanese society (a society where 90 percent of the people believe that they belong to the middle class) have noted how similar Japanese life is—particularly for people who work in large organizations and live in collective housing complexes—to the life described by W.H. Whyte in *The Organization Man.*[13]

If there is anything that distinguishes Japanese society from other societies, it is the differences in the degree and manner in which features common to all advanced industrialized nations are manifested in Japan. The first point to note is how conformity originating from traditional rural communities and the conformity characteristic of mass societies in general overlap and reinforce each other. The coexistence of tradition and modernity is also observed in other societies. Nevertheless, in Japan the conformity that traditionally characterized the rural village served as the basis upon which national conformity for modernization was forged, and this subsequently overlapped with the conformity characteristic of mass societies.

Of course, industrialization has greatly altered agricultural production modes, and mechanization and the introduction of chemical fertilizers has greatly reduced the need for cooperative labor. Nevertheless, the pressures for conformity continue to be considerable, as illustrated by the 1952 case of a family that was ostracized because their daughter had written a letter to a newspaper accusing a political candidate of election fraud in her village, thus supposedly disgracing the entire village. It is true that conformity has prevailed, but technological advances have shifted the basis of that conformity from cooperation in production to conformity in consumption. If everybody else has a color television set, the pressures to buy one yourself are practically irresistable. Every farmer feels he has to have his own small tractor to cultivate his small plot of land, even though it is obvious that it would be much more economical for the neighborhood as a group to buy one medium-sized tractor and to share it. As such, even a tractor ceases to be a tool necessary for production and becomes a form of conspicuous consumption.

When the primary basis of village conformity shifts away from productive cooperation, conformity loses its traditional agrarian features and appears in apartmenthouse complexes where there is frequent contact between neighbors and where the life style is highly standardized. Furthermore, mass communication's standardization of consumption narrows the differences between urban, rural, and other social segments. According to a 1961 BBC survey, the percentage of people who watched television at 8:00 P.M. differed markedly by viewer status: 30 percent of the upper-middle, 35 percent of the lower-middle class; and 40 percent of the lower class watching. But a 1965 survey in Japan showed a strong 45–50 percent audience irrespective of income or status differences.[14] The type of conformity which makes villagers want what their neighbors have—an extension of the traditional conformity—is very difficult to distinguish from that conformity found in mass societies, and the mass media have spread this undifferentiated conformity nationwide. The Japanese national income rose three-fold from 1952 to 1962, but the total amount of money spent on advertising increased 6.3 times in the same period, rising to 2 percent of the national income.[15] Nowadays, since advertising agencies even run election campaigns for political candidates, the people are given not only a standardized portrayal of consumer goods but a similar standardization in their politics.

If it is true that traditional values and mass values are factors strengthening conformity in modern Japan, what is paradoxical about conformity in Japan is its ties with competition. Competition in loyalty for a particular national goal has disappeared since the war, but competition between groups within Japan has actually become all the keener because it is no longer tempered by loyalty to the higher ideal of the state. Although competition within such closed in-groups as corporations and other organizations is sharply restricted in principle, the institutions of lifetime employment and seniority actually encourage competition between people of the same age cohort. For example, a given government ministry may employ 20 new career bureaucrats in a particular year. Yet there is only one vice-ministership (the highest position for a career bureaucrat) in any ministry, and the custom is for the rest of an "entering class" to resign voluntarily when one of their number becomes vice-minister. In a country like Japan, where seniority is extremely important, it is considered awkward for a vice-minister to outrank others with more seniority. A similar situation obtains in private corporations. It must be concluded that even competition within a conformity-oriented organization is, in its own way, very intense. In retail sales companies, it is competition among the branch shops which is the most intense, and in banks it is the competition among branches for it is the branch's record which determines how bright a future its manager has. This competition is so intense that it occasionally strains people beyond their limits, and some people have even committed suicide under the strain of corporate training programs. The myth of equality labels those who cannot succeed in this intense competition as either lazy or incompetent.

Let us turn next to the political function of conformity and competition in contemporary Japan. Although it is true that there is a continuity between contemporary Japanese conformity and traditional Japanese conformity, we should not therefore jump to the conclusion that this will necessarily lead to political nationalism as it did before the war. After the defeat-induced collapse of ultranationalism, and especially during Japan's rapid economic growth, the popular appetite for consumption grew as the people became increasingly interested in raising their material standard of living. Therefore, although the group orientation is as strong as ever, the group with which they identify is no longer the state but is rather first the family—specifically, the nuclear family—and second the corporation. According to a 1969 survey on "life goals," 43 percent of the respondents indicated that their goal was "to have a peaceful home life" and 17 percent cited "devotion to my work."[16] The results are pretty much the same in all similar surveys, with about half of the people primarily interested in "a happy family," and hardly anyone wanting to contribute to national goals.

The proportion of people feeling that Japan is a first-rate country increased from 41 percent in 1973 to 47 percent in 1978, and the percentage thinking that the Japanese are superior to other nationalties rose from 60 percent in 1973 to 65 percent in 1978. These findings illustrate a growing Japanese self-confidence.[17] According to one 1977 survey which asked people why they were proud of their country and of being Japanese, 36 percent mentioned "Japan's long history and traditions," 29 percent "the people's abilities and diligence," 28 percent "the natural beauty," 16 percent "the high standards of education," and 15 percent "economic affluence." Most other surveys give similar results even when conducted at different times. Therefore, it would be a mistake to conclude that the renewed Japanese confidence portends an upsurge of political or military nationalism. In fact, the same 1977 survey found, in response to the question, "Which feeling is stronger for you: wanting to do something for your country or wanting your country to do something for you?" that 48 percent wanted their country do something for them and less than 13 percent wanted to do something for their country.[18]

With regard to the question of Japanese defense, a 1976 national survey undertaken by the government showed 54 percent of the people saying that the best way to protect Japan is to maintain the combination of the Self-Defense Forces and the U.S.-Japan security treaty. But when asked what the Self-Defense Forces' most useful function has been, 74 percent mentioned relief activities in times of disaster and less than 8 percent the nation's defense.[19] Although the number of those who approve of the existence of the Self-Defense Forces has been increasing (reaching 75 percent of the interviewees in a *Yomiuri* poll conducted in April 1981), 41 percent of those approving the forces find their *raison d'être* in relief activities. Some corporations send their employees to the Self-Defense Force to give them training for specified periods of time, and although these young people feel that such training is necessary to teach them discipline, they retain their opposition to war.

Although it is true that the Japanese people are becoming more confident of themselves, Japanese society today is generally characterized by a concern first with the well-being of the family and then with the prosperity of the company that guarantees lifetime employment to ensure that family's prosperity. They are very little concerned with politics per se. Yet it is precisely this attitude of indifference that, by conforming to the existing system, contributes indirectly to the perpetuation of conservative rule. Although this attitude is conservative in not favoring sudden changes, it is not a conservatism based on ideology but what C. Wright Mills has referred to as the "conservative mood."[20]

In considering the indirect political effect that the integration of conformity and competition has on contemporary Japan, notice must also be taken of the political role played by large corporations. It has been noted elsewhere that large corporations and business associations (*zaikai*) assume, in close collaboration with the bureaucracy and the semipermanently ruling conservative party, a vital role in Japan's decision making process.[21] We shall thus concern ourselves here only with the most obvious form of collusion between business and the ruling conservative party, ironically called the Liberal Democratic party. During election campaigns, large corporations and corporate coalitions make campaign funds available to conservative candidates, at times even mobilizing their corporate machinery to get votes. The important thing here in terms of the integration between competition and conformity is that the competition among companies which prevailed during Japan's postwar economic growth resulted in the successful corporations becoming ever larger and ever more influential. This was even as these same corporations were using in-house conformity and competition in loyalty to strengthen employee loyalty and to make employees more amenable to the organizational will, thus establishing a system commanding absolute loyalty and evoking the "very best" from every worker. The traditional Japanese attitude toward organizations is not so much to make the decision-making process rational but rather to motivate members to make the maximum effort in pursuit of the organizations' established goals. To be fair, it must be added that the leading opposition party, the Japan Socialist Party, no more has an independent financial and organizational base than does the conservative party, and the Socialists must rely upon labor unions both for election campaign funds and for organizational machinery.

However, there is one new trend in Japanese organization deserving of note: the increased sense of alienation and apathy among members. Bureaucratization in huge organizations has developed without being checked by democratic procedures. This is because of the members' belief in the organic unity of the organization and because of a lack of sensitivity to the decision-making process. At the same time, the increasing bureaucratization inevitably intensifies the member's sense of alienation and apathy, and thus leads to a weakening of loyalty despite the organization's emphasis on conformity. According to a series of four studies on employee attitude at one of Japan's largest steel companies from 1952 to 1963, the percentage of people loyal to their company declined steadily from 54 percent in 1952 to 26 percent in 1963 while the percentage of employees critical of their company gradually increased from 18 percent to 44 percent. Moreover, the increase in the percentage of company-critical employees did not mean an increase in the percentage favoring the union, but the union fell out of favor just as quickly, as the union-favorable percentage dropped from 47 percent to 26 percent and the union-critical percentage rose from 26 percent to 47 percent during the same period.[22] In addition, union-favorable percentage is declining along with the company-favorable percentage because the union, being company-oriented, is quick to compromise with the company, and shares the company's alienating bureaucratic structure.

The distrust of large organizations has become increasingly apparent since the latter half of the 1960s. Nor is this distrust limited to giant corporations and unions, but extends also to political parties. Politically, this distrust was first directed against the ruling conservative party, tied as it is to big business, and then against the Japan Socialist party, supported by the big labor unions. For a while it was manifested in increased support for middle-of-the-road parties and the Communist party, but eventually all political parties came to be distrusted as part of the establishment. In the late 1970s, one in three citizens said they did not support any of the political parties, and this distrust of politics was also reflected in the increasing number of people who felt that government policies did not properly reflect the popular will.[23]

Apathy has not been the only offspring of this heightened alienation. Although not numerous, there have also been some positive results— among them the antipollution campaigns in many local communities. The emphasis on rapid economic growth generated numerous victims of pollution, yet neither the pollution-producing corporations, the labor unions, nor the political parties moved to alleviate their plight. The corporations were not only unwilling to bear the costs of preventing pollution in their lust for rapid growth, but even the unions, fearing the costs of preventing pollution would hurt their chances for ever-higher wages, often refused to speak up on the victims' behalf and occasionally were actually antagonistic. Realizing that no one would come to their aid, the local residents of some affected areas decided to launch environmental campaigns on their own. In so doing, they were very wary about alliances with the political parties, fearing that the political parties might—as in fact they sometimes did—simply use the campaign as a vote-getting device.

There are numerous citizen movements in many local communities, but the number of people participating in them is negligible compared to the number of union members. Nevertheless, they have succeeded in getting several pollution laws passed, in pressuring the government to set up the Environment Agency, and in winning several court cases fixing corporate responsibility for pollution. Also important is the fact that, in the process of carrying out these antipollution campaigns, people have developed a feel for the right of every individual to lead a healthful life and have consequently sought to establish principles to counter the Social Darwinist discrimination against those who fell by the wayside during Japan's rapid economic growth.

This trend was paralleled by an increasing rejection of the overemphasis on economic growth. Until 1969, the percentage of people supporting continued rapid growth was larger than the percentage objecting to it, but these figures reversed themselves in the 1970s until, by 1973, there were more than twice as many people objecting to it (58%) as there were supporting it (22%).[24] Furthermore, the percentage of people who said pollution was unacceptable even if necessary for industrial development increased from 27 percent in 1965 to 48 percent in 1971.[25]

But such doubts about the wisdom of rapid economic growth did not expand linearly, for people began to show renewed interest in economic development when it became apparent that there would be a prolonged recession after the 1973 oil crisis. Indeed, there was a backlash of sorts as people rapidly lost interest in social welfare. The percentage of people citing "economic growth" as the most important political issue increased from 13 percent in 1973 to 17 percent in 1978, while the percentage citing "improved social welfare" declined from 49 percent to 32 percent during the same period. Also significant on this question of identifying the most important political issue is the finding that the percentage of people citing "maintenance of law and order" rose from 13 percent in 1973 to 17 percent in 1978 while the percentage of people citing "protecting the rights of the people" declined from 12 percent to 9 percent.[26] In short, the late 1960s and early 1970s tendency to reassess rapid economic growth and to emphasize social welfare is slowly giving way to a renewed concern for economic growth and law and order.

So long as the recession continues, it is not at all certain whether or not we can recover from this reversal. The question of whether growth-oriented or welfare-oriented policies ultimately prevail depends upon the extent to which the public, particularly the young people, develops an awareness of social welfare as part of a basic human right. Although it is true that young people are becoming more aware of their rights in the sense that they do not wish to see their lives disrupted, there is no certainty that this will automatically grow into a universal concern for the rights of all individuals. Under the myth of free competition, the concept of rights can easily lead into Social Darwinism, and in a conformity-oriented society it can serve as justification for discrimination against the misfits.

As a social scientist I am extremely hesitant about making predictions concerning the future. Moreover, since all of us should endeavor to improve Japan not only for our own sake but for the sake of all people everywhere, it would ill-behoove any forecaster to make predictions which neglect the possible impact of such endeavors.

Notes

1. Robert K. Merton, *Social Theory and Social Structure,* revised ed., Glencoe, Ill., 1957, p. 126f.
2. The term is borrowed from C. Wright Mills, *The Power Elite, New York, Oxford University Press, 1956, p. 338.*
3. Morton Grodzins, *The Loyal and the Disloyal,* Chicago, University of Chicago Press, 1956, p. 19.
4. Weber finds this feature in Confucianism. *Gesammelte Aufsätze zur Religionssoziologie,* Bd. 1., Tübingen, Mohr, 1922, S.441. But this view is also related to the biocosmic approach prevailing in Japan since the mythological period—before Confucianism was introduced to Japan.
5. Kantarō Suzuki Biography Editorial Committee, *Suzuki Kantarō Den,* 1950, p. 240.
6. For details on the nature of in-groups, see Graham Summer, *Folkways,* Boston, Ginn, 1906.
7. For an account of the problem of pollution in Japan, see Norie Huddle, Michael Reich, and Nahum Stiskin, *Island of Dreams,* Brookline, Mass., Autumn Press, 1975. On the suffering that organic mercury poisoning caused (the Minamata Disease), see Masazumi Harada, "Minamata Disease as a Social and Medical Problem," *Japan Quarterly,* vol. 25, no. 1, Jan.-Mar., 1978, pp. 20–34. The situation is not very different from that of the A-Bomb victims.
8. Mircea Eliade, *Patterns in Comparative Religion,* translated by Rosemary Sheed, London, New York, Sheed and Ward, 1958.
9. Max Weber, *Gesammelte Aufsätze zur Religionssoziologie,* Bd. 2., Tübingen, Mohr., 1923, S.303-304.
10. Max Weber, *Wirtschaft und Gesellschaft, Grundriss der Verstehenden Soziologie,* Studienausgabe herausgegeben von Johannes Winckelmann, Zweiter Halbband, Berlin, Kiepernheuer & Witsch, 1964, S.854f.
11. NHK Yoron Chōsajo (ed.), *Gendai Nihonjin no Ishikikōzō,* Nihon Hōsō Shuppan Kyōkai, 1979, p.114.
12. Erich Fromm, *The Sane Society,* London, Routledge & Kegan Paul, 1956, pp. 152f.

13. William H. Whyte, Jr., *The Organization Man,* New York, Simon & Schuster, 1956; Doubleday Anchor Book, 1957.
14. Mimpōgosha Chōsakenkyūkai, *Nihon no Shichōsha,* Seibundōshinkōsha, 1966, p. 31.
15. Mimpōgosha Chōsakenkyūkai, *Nihon no Shōhisha,* Diamond-Sha, 1964, p. 58.
16. Sōrifu Kōhōshitsu (ed.), *Gekkan Yoronchōsa,* November 1969, p. 3.
17. NHK Yoron Chōsajo (ed.), *Gendai Nihonjin no Ishikikōzō,* Nihon Hōsō Shuppan Kyōkai, 1979, p. 130.
18. Sōrifu Kōhōshitsu (ed.), *Shōwa Gojūninendo Yoronchōsa Nenkan,* Ministry of Finance Printing Bureau, 1978, p. 150. A 1968 survey found that, in response to the question "What would you do if Japan were attacked by a foreign aggressor?" only 9.3 percent said they would get a gun and fight, as opposed to 28.3 percent who said they would do everything they could to stop the war.
19. Sōrifu Kōhōshitsu (ed.), *Shōwa Gojūichinendo Yoronchōsa Nenkan,* Ministry of Finance Printing Bureau, 1977, pp. 116–117.
20. C. W. Mills, op. cit., p. 360.
21. Takeshi Ishida, "Interest Groups under a Semipermanent Government Party," *The Annals of the American Academy of Political and Social Science,* vol. 413, May 1974, pp. 1–14.
22. Haruo Suzuki, "Rōdōshaishiki no Henkaku to Yoka," *Gekkan Rōdōmondai,* May 1969, p. 79.
23. According to one survey, the percentage of respondents who expressed a belief in the efficacy of politics declined from 32 percent in 1972 to 29 percent in 1978, while the ranks of the skeptical increased from 61 percent to 71 percent. *Gendai Nihonjin no Ishikikōzō,* p. 189.
24. NHK Yoron Chōsajo (ed.), *Zusetsu Sengoyoronshi,* Nihon Hōso Suppan Kyōkai, 1975, p. 195.
25. Ibid., p. 203.
26. *Gendai Nihonjin no Ishikikōzō,* op. cit., pp. 181–183.

Part II

JAPAN IN COMPARATIVE PERSPECTIVE

CHAPTER THREE

A Current Japanese Interpretation of Max Weber

I

It seems that one cannot find in Weber's writings what might be called a fully-developed "theory" of Asian society. Weber never examined societies in Asia with the idea of applying to them a specific model which might enable us to discern their characteristics.

According to Weber, Chinese and Indian society have the common feature of identifying the social order with the natural order. Both have "exemplary prophecy" in contrast to the "ethical prophecy" of Persia and Arabia (Zoroaster and Muhammad); in this respect they clearly differ from Occidental societies. However, between themselves these two Asian societies differ in that Chinese society is value-oriented towards acceptance of the world *(Weltbejahung)* whereas Indian society is value-oriented towards rejection of the world *(Weltablehnung)*. With regard to rejection of the world, the Occidental tradition of Christianity also has much in common with the Indian tradition, though Christianity falls under the subcategory of control-of-the-world *(Weltbeherrschung)* while Indian culture is based on escape-from-the-world *(Weltflucht)*. It therefore would be both impertinent and very misleading to find consistency in Weber's views on Asia, where Weber himself found variety.

As Weber made clear in his introduction to *The Sociology of Religion,* his central concern was to explain why modern capitalism developed, and why it only developed in the Occident. Such a concern logically led him to place emphasis on an analysis of the process by which differences arose between Occident and non-Occident, the latter being a term which may be taken to represent the Orient in the broad sense. (As mentioned above, Weber wisely did not regard the non-Occident, or Orient, as a homogeneous unit.)

51

According to Weber, it is impossible to explain by a simple sequence of cause and effect why modern capitalism was able to develop only in the Occident. The question had to be approached from various directions by taking into account a variety of ideas *(Ideen)*, social strata *(soziale Schichten)* and states of interests *(Interessenlage)*. In some Asian societies, there are those elements which, typologically, can also be found in Occidental societies. On the other hand, certain Asian societies were not necessarily precluded from developing in the same way as Occidental societies. Thus, Weber showed himself opposed to economic determinism such as that of Kautzky. Moreover, he was never the cultural or religious determinist he was often unjustifiably criticized as being. The practice of treating the non-Occidental world as a unified entity and enumerating its "essential" characteristics is decidedly not Weber's methodology.

Instead of going into Weber's discussion of Oriental societies, I would seek here to throw light on the manner in which Weber's theories have been understood in Japan, in contrast to the way Weber has been understood in the West. What are the concerns which have motivated Japanese social scientists to adopt Weberian theory? What aspects have come to the fore in the Japanese understanding of Weber? What is the relationship between them and the socio-historical conditions existing in Japan?

Mention must first be made of the great popularity Weber enjoys among Japanese social scientists. One hundred years since his birth and less than fifty years since his death in 1920, the number of monographs and articles on Weber written in Japanese amounts to nearly one thousand. Looking at this massive list of documents, I was dismayed to realize how few I had read. This led me to doubt whether I was really qualified to comment on Japanese studies of Weber. Perhaps, the most I can do here is to make but a few points in a limited area of this field.[1]

Recently I was given an opportunity of serving as one of the chairmen at a symposium celebrating the centenary of Weber's birth. More than two hundred experts from various fields of study convened for a two-day discussion.[2] The impressions gathered on that occasion helped me a great deal in forming an overview of Japanese studies of Weber today. Before examining the main characteristics of these studies, however, a historical perspective of Weberian studies in the context of the Japanese intellectual climate may prove of some value.

Up until the early 1930s, Japan had experienced a stage where the introduction of Weberian theory was of tremendous significance. The method of "interpretive sociology" *(verstehende Soziologie)*, the theory of freedom from value-judgment, and the theory of ideal types were among the first that were brought to the attention of Japanese intellectuals. They provided a stimulus which enabled Japanese social scientists, previously strongly influenced by German *Staatswissens-chaften,* to move from the position of statist policy studies to one of liberating the social sciences. Conversely, once Japanese social scientists had been so oriented, Weber's thesis of freedom from value-judgment so readily attracted their attention. Still, the Japanese image of Weber at that time was little more than that of an extraordinarily erudite Neo-Kantian scholar.

In the latter half of the 1930's, when Japan reached the fascist/militarist stage, studies of Weber began to have a special meaning in the intellectual climate of the time. Typical of that stage for Japan, was a then fashionable slogan, "Overcoming Modernity." This slogan had a twofold implication:

In the first aspect, it was to mobilize anti-Western sentiments among the masses by equating "modernity" with "Western modernity." These sentiments comprised both policy questions (opposition to Western imperialism) and emotional factors (yellow/white antipathy). All these factors had the common feature of anti-Western thinking. As Professor R. Bendix points out, Japan was characterized by a much greater homogeneity than Germany, where the development of capitalism was likewise late, so that she reacted highly sensitively to the increase of heterogeneity attendant upon urbanization.[3] There was a strong tendency often to regard any menace to internal homogeneity as an evil brought about by the Western impact. These sentiments became further intensified by Japan's growing isolation in world affairs.

In the second aspect, subtly distinguishable from the first, was the tendency to disapprove of modern elements in Japan—liberalism, parliamentarism, constitutionalism, etc.—as well as of the social phenomena resulting from urbanization. Politically, this tendency comprised those elements which sought to weaken parliament and the political parties. Intellectually, it was a rejection of modern Western thought, which had already exerted great influence on Japan, by labeling it anti-Japanese, or destructive of the fundamental character of the national polity. There was even the discovery of a menace to the Japanese tradition in the consequences of urbanization.

In the intellectual climate of the time, Weber's theory also possessed a twofold meaning: First, the spirit of modern capitalism and the subsequent modern state were far more rational than traditional, precapitalist, forms of domination. In Japan, what was really at issue was not the overcoming of modernity, but the need to create modern social relations. Second, the Japanese character which the exponents of "overcoming modernity" praised so highly should have been regarded as a deterrent to increasing rationalism, as Weber himself pointed out in his *Sociology of Religion,* volume 1 (especially in the chapter on Confucianism and Taoism). The results of Weber's analysis of Oriental societies and the types of domination he described in his *Economy and Society* eventually provided for Japanese social scientists a very effective weapon for analyzing their own society.

The process by which the Japanese value system was rapidly losing rationality due to the growth of fascism had the effect of impressing upon the small number of Japanese social scientists the correctness of Weber's theory. At a time when his theory was censured as a "dead science" by his countryman Othmar Spann, that same theory was inspiring social scientists in Japan. At that time, one of them, Tadashi Fukutake, responding to Spann, declared that Weber's theory was alive, and would not perish, because of the importance of Weber's method of "freedom from value judgment" *(Wertfreiheit).* Indeed, in protecting the independence of studies in the face of increasing suppression from a militaristic regime, the Japanese social scientists were provided with the best possible base for a methodology based on freedom from value judgment.

With regard to "overcoming modernity," mention must be made of the relationship between Weber and Marx in Japan. It was after the war that Marxism, fully and candidly expressed, gained importance as a systematic methodology. The question of Marxism will be taken up later in the discussion of the circumstances following the war. It must be pointed out here, however, that even before the war—before it was suppressed by the fascist government—Marxism had a strong influence among the intellectuals. Marxism was connected with "overcoming modernity" in the sense that Western modernity meant bourgeois society, the overcoming of which being the major task of Marxism. Japanese Marxists, especially members of the Communist Party and, after their suppression, their intellectual successors held to a two-stage theory of revolution: That is, what Japan needed now was a bourgeois-democratic revolution; the socialist revolution would only come after the first had run its course. So long as they held this position, these Marxists shared, for a time, a common target with those who held with Weber and sought to achieve Western modernity (i.e., capitalism) in Japan. The all-out disapproval of the emperor system among the Marxists had a certain affinity with the Weberians' criticism of factors which prevented the growth of rationalism from growing in Oriental societies. Also, the fact that both Marxists and Weberians suffered, physically and psychologically, under the emperor system allowed for a greater affinity between the two groups.

At the same time, the Marxists' desire to end bourgeois society and their opposition to the "invasion of Asia by the Western imperialist powers" also allowed for an affinity between them and the exponents of "overcoming modernity." The ultranationalists laid emphasis on aspects highly particular to Japan, while the Marxists were oriented towards the universalist goal of the liberation of mankind. This major difference must not be overlooked. Some Marxists, however, while using the phraseology of "overcoming modernity," considered it no more than the "language of slaves." That is, they felt forced to use this terminology to avoid right wing repression. Some Marxists, however, sought to justify the Pacific War (i.e. World War II) as serving the dual purpose of aiding (1) the Asian nations' revolt against Western imperialism and (2) the proletarian push to overcome bourgeois society. In both these cases, Weber conflicted somewhat with Marx. In this respect, the "converted" Marxists formed an affinity with the ultranationalistic elements seeking to overcome modernity. It seemed to them that both German fascism and Soviet socialism represented the defeat of Western bourgeois modernity by the historical process. The German-Soviet treaty of nonaggression supported such a belief. In the period prior to the war, genuine Marxists (i.e., those not converted to ultra-nationalism) were put into jail, and, like many others, effectively silenced. As the militarist system tightened its control, even silence was no longer enough; they now had to constantly *prove* their loyalty to Japan by positive action. In this atmosphere, seeking to reconcile their beliefs with the will to survive, many of them joined hands with the ultra-nationalistic exponents of "overcoming modernity," by demanding that modern-Western (bourgeois) society be overcome.

Therefore, until the postwar period, when Marxism was granted full citizenship in our intellectual world, the problem of Weber versus Marx remained largely unresolved.

II

The changes which took place in Japan's intellectual climate following the defeat initially took the form of a reaction against the ideology behind the war; "overcoming modernity" was one aspect of it. The lost war and the Occupation diffused the dichotomy of feudal and modern values. This was often identified with the dichotomy of new Western values and traditional Japanese values. It was regarded as necessary that Japan create modern Western social relations and reject feudal tradition. Social scientists also found themselves with greater freedom in such an atmosphere, but their primary concern was how they could analyze effectively the Japanese militarist system in order to permanently destroy it from the roots upward. There was an urgent need for satisfactory answers to the questions as to how the Japanese militarist system had been able to dominate, why it could not have been checked from within, and why the emperor system could enjoy so strong a unifying influence that it could pry into individual minds and generate blind loyalty.

The emperor's political prerogatives and the privileged organs surrounding the Throne, such as the Privy Council and the House of Peers, were abolished. The armed services were also abolished. The *zaibatsu* were dissolved. Large scale landlordism was discontinued. Was this sufficient to bring about Western-style modernity? Those institutions had been so clearly defective and completely discredited that criticism was naturally concentrated on them. When this old machinery was destroyed, however, doubts grew strong as to whether the "revolution by law" based solely on Occupation policy could overcome defects traditionally inherent in Japanese society. Social scientists began to focus their concern on the social relations and behavior patterns which had supported—and been supported by—the old structure. These, they believed, had not been greatly changed by the "revolution by law." It was against this background of increasing concern that the name of Weber began to appear even more in the works of Japanese social scientists. In seeking a deep analysis of the characteristic features of Japanese society, in a critical fashion, it seemed that the methods which Weber used for his analysis of Asian societies would provide an effective tool. This was especially true of the methodology of *Economy and Society,* particularly his discussion of patrimonialism.

Mention must be made of three scholars who were to play a major role in making Weber's name familiar to almost all students of the social sciences in postwar Japan. These scholars sought to understand Weber not as an alternative, but as a complement, to Marx. Not only did they make Weber's name widely known in Japan but Japanese interpretations of Weber began to take a definite shape in the works of these scholars: Hisao Ōtsuka, specializing in British economic history; Masao Maruyama, in political science; and Takeyoshi Kawashima, in the sociology of law. There can be no doubt among Japanese intellectuals that these three are indispensable to any discussion of the social sciences of postwar Japan. Weber's influence upon them varies both in quantity and quality, but the Weberian theory provides one of the most important components of their analytical framework.

Hisao Ōtsuka came to create his unique views on British economic history through studying Weber's *The Protestant Ethic and the Spirit of Capitalism* and other works, along with various works by Marx, particularly his *Capital* (especially volume 1, chapter 24). He sought to combine the Weberian theory of types with the Marxian theory of stages of development to prove the most effective use of it in historical analysis. His idea of the pattern of development was an offshoot of such an application of Weber's theory. He developed Marx's materialist view of history away from mere economic determinism in the narrow sense (Marx himself was not this sort of economic determinist) and located it in the Weberian perspective of interests (*Interessen*) and ideas (*Ideen*), thereby emphasizing the importance of ethos. Although he learned from *The Protestant Ethic* how emphasis should be laid on ethos, his originality lies in the fact that he related it to Marx's theory of local communities. That is, he took note of the relationship between ethos and the most basic structure of social relations (communities). Ōtsuka has always had, behind his analysis of European economic history, a strong motivation—his concern to appraise critically Japanese society; in fact, even when he is writing on Europe, it is possible to read his criticism of Japanese society between the lines. Such motivation shows Ōtsuka to be in a position similar to that of Weber who himself was once criticized for being an Anglophile. Weber valued highly the role of religious sects in America—as made clear in *Protestant Sects and the Spirit of Capitalism* which he wrote after his visit to the United States in 1904—and compared it to Germany after Lutheranism.

During the war Masao Maruyama analyzed the history of political thought in Japan under Tokugawa feudalism, influenced by Weber's "Confucianism and Taoism," Hegel's *Philosophy of World History*, G. Lukács' *History and Class Consciousness*, and the various works of Marx. His motivation here was intellectual resistance to the trend of the times as represented by "Overcoming Modernity." In his method of unifying Marx's and Hegel's views of historical development and Weber's theory of types, Maruyama had something in common with Ōtsuka. After the war, criticism of the privileged political machinery became insufficient as this machinery was now (at least officially) extinct; Maruyama then conducted studies of the psychology and behavior of Japanese militarism which many Japanese intellectuals found extremely interesting and stimulating. Like Ōtsuka, who took note of the importance of ethos, Maruyama sought to bring to light the relationship between consciousness and society, just as Weber had done in his own fashion. Maruyama's consistent concern was to throw light on those factors which prevented rationalism from growing in Japan. Since some of his important works have been translated into English, interested readers may refer directly to his work rather than subject themselves to a simplified description here.[4]

In the case of Takeyoshi Kawashima, a pioneer in the study of the sociology of law, the influence of both Weber and Marx is remarkable. In an attempt to clarify the relationship between law and social structure, under the influence of Marx's *Capital* and *German Ideology*, he sought to inquire into the "familistic structure of Japanese society" by means of Weber's analysis of patrimonialism and "sociology of law" (*Rechtssoziologie*) as found in *Economy and Society*.[5] In his *Theory of the Law of Property,* his discussion of the economic basis of modern property rights was influenced by Marx, and his analysis of legal consciousness by Weber; he sought to bring to light the characteristics of modern property law through unifying these two systems of thought.

None of these three social scientists is regarded in Japan as a Marxist. There has been a greater tendency in Japan than in the West for Weber and Marx to mean a combination of methods rather than a choice between them. The motivation underlying the combining of Weber and Marx was the desire of our scholars to most effectively analyze Japan's traditional society. The method common to the three was to make effective use of Weber with regard to the problem of historical development, by paying greater attention to the problem of consciousness or ethos than Marxists had done hitherto. They were able to develop such a problem-consciousness and methodology out of their personal experience of Japanese militarism, and the driving need to understand how and why such a militalist system could emerge and dominate Japan. They thus had a strong influence on both their contemporaries and their juniors.

Emphasizing the strong relationship between Weber and Marx, sociologist Kazuhiko Sumiya has said that today we should talk about Marx-Weber instead of Max Weber! He contrasted such a tendency in Japan with the tendency in the United States to consider Weber in connection with Parsons. The strong Japanese tendency toward the combination of Marx and Weber has never really eliminated the recurring problem of occasionally having to choose between them. It is obvious that Weber is appreciably different from Marx in method and in underlying orientation. Those who have been strongly influenced by

Weber were criticized as "modernists" by Marxists. Weberians uphold bourgeois society as the supreme goal while Marxists demand that such a society be overturned in the movement towards socialism. Another criticism by Marxists is that Weberians have underrated the importance of foundation (*Unterbau*) in materialism by laying emphasis on ethos or consciousness. Since the phenomenon Daniel Bell called "the end of ideology" has begun to be generally recognized, Marxist criticism of Weberians is now weaker than before.[6] Nevertheless, in combining the methods of Weber and Marx certain incongruous elements in the two systems still pose difficult problems. If one seeks to rid oneself of Marx's monolithic monism in favor of a pluralist point of view, one might lose sight of the main characteristic of Marxism, which is a total and structural analysis of society. On the Weber side, the method of deriving types from the variety of viewpoints may well lead to becoming, in Weber's own words, a "soulless specialist." Weber himself foresaw this possibility and called it tragic. The need to free ourselves from monolithic monism, balanced by the need to understand society as a whole, leaves us in a permanent *aporia*. I am of the opinion that we can expect social science to progress from the unlimited efforts we make to solve this problem while we must always bear in mind the tension between these two needs.

While Marxist criticism of the Weberians (or those strongly influenced by Weber) is waning, there is another tendency which is recently increasing among Weber's critics. It is that they are "modernists," or "Occidentalists," and excessively critical of Japanese tradition because of their "theory of absence,"—that the West has had something in its history which Japan has "lacked." This new criticism is derived from the recent economic prosperity of Japan and the subsequent national confidence, aspiration for national prestige, and popular feelings for regaining national identity. These critics, who are still to produce any sophisticated kind of work in the field of social science, have a taint of anti-intellectualism and represent, for the present, only a small trend. Because of their social basis, however, their future influence will be worth noticing. Ironically, the recent tendency among American scholars studying Japan to see Japan's rapid modernization as an *exception* among non-Occidental societies has the effect of further encouraging these critics of the Weberians. For they now turn the Americans' words around and emphasize the significance of those traditions *peculiar* to Japan, and take the next step: a positive reassessment of Japan's past, including World War II. It is presumable that such a new tendency may grow among those Japanese social scientists who are susceptible to any new trend of social science in the West.

(This was seen in the precedent of the ideology of nazism being utilized to denounce liberalism and other ideas originating in the West.)

A theory may be unfolded that places more emphasis on technology in society than on social structure or ethos (which Weberians emphasize) a tendency among American social scientists who are reassessing Japan. In that case, the romantic traditionalism of those admirers of Japan's past may be hidden under the highly sophisticated theorization of technology.

III

In the foregoing, I have roughly traced historical changes in the understanding of Weber in Japan in relation to the intellectual climate in the country. In the following, an attempt will be made to summarize some characteristics of interpretations of Weber in Japan. In trying to put the discussion in a proper perspective, due to the fact that I am only familiar with a small number of the studies on Weber which have appeared so far, only a very brief and necessarily incomplete survey is possible. The discussion will be centered inevitably around the ideas of the three scholars previously mentioned. The views expressed at the symposium to celebrate the centenary of Weber's birth, including those of many social scientists from generations younger than those three, have also provided much important material. However, the following characterization may not be applicable to the majority of Japanese studies on Weber.

First, mention must be made of the motivational approach which permeates the Japanese understanding of Weber. Marianne Weber's biography of her husband has been translated into Japanese, as well as many of Weber's works. The biography has been widely read among Japanese intellectuals concerned with the historical background, and the intentions, of Weber's work. Underlying their concern, perhaps, is their sympathy with Weber's ardent quest for rationality in a Germany which appeared to have fallen far behind other countries in terms of culture. In this sense, the image of Weber in Japan seems quite different from that in Germany, where many of his countrymen have sought to understand Weber against a historical background and have regarded him as a "Nationalist" holding controversial political opinions or even as a chauvinistic imperialist. This was indicated in the atmosphere surrounding the German Congress of Sociology of 1964, held at Heidelberg, devoted to the theme of "Max Weber and Contemporary Sociology."[7] This difference of emphasis between Japanese and German scholars is attributable perhaps to the distance between the two countries; perhaps to the fact that we in Japan are, of course, not as sensitive to the influence of Weber in Germany as the Germans themselves are; perhaps because of the role Weber inadvertently played in Japan's militarist era.

A number of Western scholars, particularly Americans, note the strong concern of Japanese intellectuals for motivation, and the importance of "problem-consciousness," (a phrase difficult to translate into English) to their critical ideological position in relation to Japanese society and government. They feel that Japanese social scientists are more critical of their own institutions than they need to be. Yet it ought to be pointed out that such an attitude has its own historical reasons. It originates in the great difficulty they experienced in retaining their objectivity during the war. Japanese militarism not only sought to control social science by means of physical force, it had a subtle but strong tendency towards incorporating the social scientists themselves, often unwittingly, into the value system of the Empire under the overwhelming pressure of national consensus. After the war they felt much guilt and remorse. This explains why, in the postwar study of Weber's idea of freedom from values (*Wertfreiheit*), emphasis was placed on the effort to reveal the value premise of the social scientist, a premise often hidden or unconscious. To achieve *freedom from values,* in Weber's sense, does not mean to lose value-judgment at all, for it is impossible to eliminate value-judgments. If one claims that one has done so, then he is unconsciously lying to himself and others; this, of course, is a dangerous condition. Rather, *freedom from values* means that the social scientist is, as far as is possible, conscious of his own ideas, values, and value-judgments and is thus able to control the results of analysis obtaining from such value-judgment. While retaining values themselves, the social scientist can thus eliminate wishful thinking deriving from value-judgment in order to obtain an analysis free from bias.

In brief, Weber's idea of *freedom from value* is not one of excluding the problem of values from the arena of social science; on the contrary, the problem of value has great importance for Weber in the following two senses. First, in order to set up a problem or a viewpoint, a value standpoint is needed in the first place. It is therefore important to make a free choice of the value standpoint needed to set up a viewpoint, to be *consciously* aware of it, so as to be able to call it into question. Second, there is the meaning of value as an object of analysis. While Weber had certain factors in common with Marx in that he recognized the situation (state) of interests (*Interessenlage*) to be the propelling power in historical development, he emphasized the importance of idea, value, or what he called the world image (*Weltbild*) which he thought determined the direction in which interests make history advance. This was the very reason why Weber was led to prepare that voluminous work, *The Sociology of Religion.* We have already noticed, in the Japanese understanding of Weber, the tendency to emphasize his strong concern for value as shown in that work.

An example of the Japanese understanding of Weber's *freedom from values* and its strong influence on Japanese social scientists is the sense of discord felt among many of them concerning the recent studies of modernization based on the behavioral approach in the United States. As the behavioral approach, developing fast in the United States, has been extended to the field of comparative studies, efforts have been made to find common criteria for modernization going beyond the ideological differences between the capitalist and socialist systems. Consequently, attempts have been made to determine the degree of modernization by such objective, easily quantifiable, measurements, as per capita income, literacy rate, and degree of exposure to mass communication media. It is true that these attempts may produce far more objective results than ideological criteria, but many social scientists in Japan entertain apprehensions that such studies of modernization underrate the importance of values. This in turn is related to the above discussion regarding the importance for Weber of values. While sociological conditions are easy to quantify and apparently are an important factor in history, the *problem of values,* which plays the significant role in determining the direction of historical development, is also a worthy object of social science. There is also the problem of the self-consciousness of social scientists themselves with respect to value-judgment. Many Japanese social scientists have misgivings about the lack of self-examination and the tendency to accept statistics obtained as if they had no value premise at all. If the figures are obtained without bearing in mind value-judgment, then it is only an unconscious dependence on a given value-judgment—which may be a uniquely personal one, or a value-judgment prevailing in society. If Japanese social scientists are criticized because they appear too critical of their own society, they might well retaliate by stressing the completely opposite tendency among American social scientists, who produce "policy science" i.e. "scientific" research supporting government policies.

Regarding the importance of motivation and value, one should point out a second characteristic in the Japanese understanding of Weber, i.e., the importance of irrational factors in Weber's idea of increasing rationality in society. The Weber centenary symposium chose the historical meaning of Weber in such specific fields as sociology, juris-prudence and history, for its first-day sessions, and the common theme of increasing rationality (*Rationalisierung*) for the second day. Space does not permit a detailed discussion, but, compared with American studies of modernization, the method of grasping the idea of increasing rationality shown at the conference had certain discernible characteristics. If bold simplification may be permitted, it can be said that when secularization is referred to as a criterion of modernization, one presupposes a unilinear view of progress based on a gradual decrease in irrational elements in inverse proportion to a gradual increase in rational elements. On the contrary, in understanding Weber's increasing rationality, we must attach importance to the different types of religious prophets or the role which charisma plays in the course of increasing rationality. In considering the emergence of modern states and the modern legal order, stress was laid on the role of the idea of natural law as a charismatic sanctification of the logos. Such a tendency has its own historical reasons.

In the case of Japan, where there has been a strong Confucian tradition of what Weber called "rationalism of order," religion had played only a minor part, and therefore the theory of evolution was adopted with little resistance from religion.

Opposition to the idea of natural law, in Japan, took the form of emphasizing the judgment that this idea was an illusion. Against such a historical background, it is clear that the tendency to emphasize irrational elements in the course of increasing rationalism in Japan has a sound historical basis. Some behavioralists, accepting the American theory of modernization, tend to connect a unilinear model of progress, such as that mentioned above, with Weber's theory of types, and thereby hold that modernization represents the process of development from traditional domination, through charismatic domination, to legal domination. The previous reference in this article to the tendency in Japan regarding a historical understanding of Weber's theory of types is not to be interpreted as supportive of the unilinear interpretation. On the contrary, what is meant here is that one can only provide an effective means of understanding history in motion if Weber's types are taken not merely as fixed and immovable patterns but as mutually conflicting and yet interchangeable factors. To cite an example, in Weber's theory, "The contrast between the emergency character of charismatic leadership and the everyday routine of legal and traditional domination also has implication for the problem of succession."[8] In interpreting the American party system Weber used the two types: (1) the charisma of the president, and (2) the management of party organization—and was able to reach a dynamic understanding of the historical development of the party system. This was because he perceived the interaction of those two types and the transformation of charisma into everyday routine and vice versa.[9] A view of Weber which holds to a unidirectional development from charismatic to legal domination offers a poor analysis of the dynamic process of history.

Here, a tendency in American social science has been contrasted with a tendency in Japan. This is not to make a general comparison of social science in the two countries. In America, we can point to, for instance, Robert Bellah, who studies Japan by following Weber's approach, with special emphasis on the problem of the value system.[10] Here I have taken up only *one* tendency among American social scientists, simply for the sake of contrast, in order to clarify characteristics in the Japanese interpretations of Weber. The reader is reminded that a general characterization of American social science or a comprehensive study of interpretations of Weber among American social scientists is far beyond the scope of this article.[11]

IV

Some mention must be made of the Japanese social scientist's understanding of Max Weber's studies of Asian societies. One characteristic is the importance they attach to cultural peculiarity, or value system in relation to social structure. As pointed out earlier, Weber did not treat Asian societies as a coherent entity. When he posed the question of why modern capitalism developed only in the West, he logically proceeded by a method of analysis designed to make clear the difference between Occident and non-Occident. On this point, however, he did not take a single-tracked view, and is not in agreement with the views of some behaviorist studies on underdeveloped or developing countries today. He said, in effect, that these areas fall behind the West only in the degree of development. These latter studies, which compare the degree of development by means of quantifiable elements, tend to ignore cultural differences. Of course, if the cultural uniqueness of each region of the world alone is emphasized, the result will be a cultural relativism or a total defiance of the possibility of making comparison between cultures. Therefore Weber's own method is very effective in that he makes multilateral comparisons by means of various categories, such as "ethical" vs. "exemplary" prophecies, or acceptance-of-the-world vs. rejection-of-the-world, while clarifying the cultural peculiarities of India, China and other areas in light of their historical background. Special attention is paid to the matter of world image and value system which have a considerable bearing on how a specific course of historical development is chosen.[12] Japan today, for example, is distinct from other Asian societies in terms of material achievements, and in this respect she stands rather close (i.e., rather similar) to Occidental societies. If, however, emphasis is laid on the value system, there is no denying that she has many elements in common with other Asian societies. One example is the tendency to identify the natural order with the social order. This, of course, does not mean to say that Japanese society is on the whole similar to other Asian societies. Weber avoided this pitfall and rejected an all-inclusive characterization of Asian society.

Another aspect of the Japanese understanding of Weber's view of Asian societies is the appreciation of how he relates his theory of these societies to that of Occidental societies. This is a logical requirement in the light of what was said previously: Weber was conscious of the problem of why modern capitalism developed only in the Occident. I have noticed how this has affected Japanese understanding of Weber, because of the manner in which these two areas are related in the Japanese mind. For social scientists living in an Asian society such as Japan, and who regard Weber's analysis of Asian societies as highly suggestive, the "problem of Asian societies" is not remote; it is their own. For Weber, too, the problem of the Asian was something more than a subject chosen out of esoteric curiosity. It was, rather, an area which he needed to explore in order to discover why modern capitalism developed in the West, and not in other areas. In Weber's eyes those factors, which were disadvantageous to the development of capitalism in Asian societies were not alien to the West, but had been overcome in the West under certain historical conditions. We, social scientists living in an Asian society, are required to discover and analyze the conditions needed for overcoming those factors. Japan today, if compared with other societies in Asia, is a highly developed country. In this respect she shares various difficulties faced by modern Western capitalist countries. Japanese social scientists, however, cannot be complacent with the idea that as Japan becomes more thoroughly Westernized, her difficulties will be removed. Investigations need to be made as to what factors should be encouraged to grow and what difficulties need to be avoided in Japanese society. In considering this problem, it must be remembered that Weber was never optimistic about the future of the West. He did note the brighter side of the modern West in the contrast of Confucianism and puritanism, the spontaneous growth of capitalism in England and the positive role of clubs and religious sects in America. At the same time, however, he emphasized the possibility of bureaucratization as one phase of rationalization or as a thorough structuring of society leading to an irrational autocracy by organization. When he says, "While the puritan wanted to be a man with a calling, we are compelled to be one," Weber was fearful that in the West the "soulless specialist" would become the dominant image of man. Here lies the reason why Japanese social scientists must, in analyzing their own society, bring into question his theory not only of Oriental but also of Occidental societies. The same must be said of our collegues in other Asian societies, also.

One thing this writer would like to note here is that Weber, living in Germany, started his studies out of profound reflections on the problems of his own society. Apparently this enabled him both to criticize the intellectual tradition and social structure of Germany following Lutheranism and at the same time find critical insights into the trend of development by means of typical examples of modern society in the West. This point is formulated into a theory in Weber's own sociology of religion, and is called by a young Japanese social scientist, Hiroshi Orihara, the "Weberian theory of marginal areas." It is summarized in Weber's writings when he says: "Rarely have entirely new religious conceptions originated in the respective centers of rational cultures. . . . To be sure this never occurred without the influence and impact of a neighboring rational civilization." For this reason, Weber adds, " . . prerequisite to new religious conceptions is that man must not yet have unlearned how to face the course of the world with questions of his own. Precisely the man distant from the great culture centers has cause to do so when their influence begins to affect or threaten his central interests." He concludes, "The possibility of questioning the meaning of the world presupposes the capacity to be astonished about the course of events."[13]

It is evident that Weber is not setting forth geographical, or any other, determinism. What is in question here is not merely whether or not a society is far away from the center of "civilization." Rather it is the process which takes place when a society far from a center of rational culture begins to question the meaning of world affairs through cultural contact and the reexamination of tradition; this helps to establish, in Weber's phraseology, the Archimedean leverage point and opens the way for an original attitude about the meaning of the world. This process could also take place within the same geographical area as seen in the case of the origin of "proletarian or pariah intellectualism" typified by Weber.

The theory to which Weber gave birth by reconsidering the West while living in what he may have considered a comparatively backward area of Western society, and by deliberately selecting a viewpoint beyond the West, has been infinitely suggestive to Japanese social scientists who live in a country where Westernization is progressing, yet is both geographically and culturally far away from the "center" of the West. It requires them once again to ask fundamental questions about their own tradition and Western tradition with a view to arriving at new interpretations. It is against such a background that Japanese interpretations of Weber came into being. The influence of these Japanese social scientists may not always have been fruitful in the past; it may be far off in the future when we can talk about success in our efforts. But even the modest fruit of such efforts can be, as this writer sincerely hopes, reinterpreted, and progress made through an increasing dialogue with social scientists in other societies.

Notes

1. To do a thorough job of discussing the studies on Max Weber in Japan, the author would have to dedicate much space and energy to a good number of social scientists and their works covering more than half a century. Such professors as K. Ōkōchi, Y. Deguchi, H. Aoyama, T. Toda, S. Uehara, K. Sera, S. Masuda, Y. Horigome, and K. Odaka, E. Andō, Y. Uchida, R. Takeda, A. Baba, and Y. Atoji are well known for their disregard of the differences among the scientific disciplines employed in their work, and for producing some careful developments of Weber's thesis and profound critical comments on him. However, it is a task beyond the ability of the present writer. In this paper specific attention has been drawn to a limited number of social scientists only in relation to some characteristics of the intellectual climate in each historical stage; in other words, with respect to the character of the times and expressed in the slogan "overcoming modernity." From this limited point of view, some characteristics in the understanding of Max Weber's world of thought might be made clear and at the same time some important points in studies of Max Weber remain untouched. In this respect the author must apologize to the reader and to the numerous scholars of Max Weber in Japan.
2. The papers presented at the conference were published later. See Hisao Ōtsuka (ed.), *Max Weber Kenkyū (Studies in Max Weber)*, Tokyo University Press, 1965.
3. Reinhard Bendix, *Nation Building and Citizenship*, New York, London, John Wiley & Sons, 1964, p. 179.
4. Masao Maruyama, *Thought and Behaviour in Modern Japanese Politics*, London, Cambridge University Press, 1963. For a review of this book, see Ronald P. Dore in *New Left Review*, May-June 1964.
5. These studies resulted in the publication of the well-known work: *Nihon Shakai no Kazoku-teki Kōsei (The Familistic Structure of Japanese Society)*, Tokyo, Gakusei-shobō, 1948.
6. Daniel Bell, *The End of Ideology*, Glencoe, Ill., The Free Press, 1960.

7. "Letter from Heidelberg: Storm over Max Weber," *Encounter*, Aug. 1964, pp. 57–59.
8. R. Bendix, *Max Weber: an Intellectual Portrait*, New York, Doubleday, 1962, p. 301.
9. Max Weber, *Wirtschaft und Gesellschaft*, 4 Aufl., T.C.B. Mohr, Tübingen, 1956, S.768.
10. Robert N. Bellah, *Tokugawa Religion, the Values of Pre-Industrial Japan*, Glencoe, Ill., The Free Press, 1957. For the author's acceptance of Masao Maruyama's criticism of his error in applying Weber's idea of "inner-world asceticism" *(innerweltliche Askese)* to Japanese history, see, Bellah, "Reflections on the Protestant Ethic Analogy in Asia," *Journal of Social Issues*, 19, 1963.
11. For American studies of Weber, reference must be made to Talcott Parsons, *The Structure of Social Action; a Study in Social Theory with Special Reference to a Group of Recent European Writers*, Glencoe, Ill., The Free Press, 1949, and the subsequent works by the same author; the Introduction in Hans H. Gerth and C. Wright Mills, *From Max Weber: Essays in Sociology*, Oxford University Press, New York, 1946; the Introduction in Max Rheinstein, *Max Weber on Law in Economy and Society*, Cambridge, Mass., Harvard University Press, 1954; and Reinhard Bendix, *Max Weber: an Intellectual Portrait*, New York, Doubleday, 1962. Interpretations of Weber appearing in those works are different from the tendency in American social science referred to in the text and show an excellent understanding of him, from which we Japanese social scientists have learned many things.
12. Gerth and Mills gave a brilliant account of Weber's theory by defining this as "the theory of ideas and interests." (Gerth and Mills, *op. cit.*, pp. 63–64.)
13. Max Weber, *Gesammelte Aufsätze zur Religionssoziologie*, Mohr, Tübingen, Bd. 3, 1923, S.320–321. The translation of the quotations follow Hans H. Gerth and Don Martindale trans. and eds., *Ancient Judaism*, Glencoe, Ill., The Free Press, 1952, pp. 206–207.

CHAPTER FOUR

Westernism and Western "Isms"

I

When Japan and other Asian societies were confronted with the advance of Western powers in the mid-nineteenth century, the first thing which struck the leaders in those societies was the surprising superiority of the West in terms of armament. It was natural, therefore, that efforts were concentrated on introducing Western military technology as quickly as possible. In both China and Japan the first stage was the introduction of Western technology while still maintaining Oriental values. Slogans such as *wakon yōsai* (Japanese spirit, Western means) or *chung t'i hsi yung* (Chinese essentials, Western means) reflect this type of thinking. However, much quicker than the Chinese intellectual elite—complacent in its belief in China as the "central empire,"—the Japanese intellectuals became aware that the strength of the Western powers was not only in their arms but also in their institutions and value systems. The most important reason for Masanao Nakamura, who translated John Stuart Mill's *On Liberty* in 1871, becoming a Christian and recommending the Emperor be baptized was his belief that the basis of Western wealth and power was Christianity. But whether he really understood the transcendental element in Christianity is questionable. For Nakamura, Christianity was basically the same as Confucianism, for "respecting heaven and loving people." Later he returned to Confucianism without seeing any need for a formal recantation.

Cultural tension between East and West was a highly complex dilemma for Japanese intellectuals. It is a question whether early Japanese Westernizers were fearful of losing their cultural identity. When one discusses the interplay of foreign influence and traditional culture in Japan, one must always be aware that, depending on the period, what is considered cultural tradition may already include certain foreign influences. As early as the sixth century, Japan was introducing foreign elements from Chinese, Indian (Buddhist, by way of China and Korea), and other cultures. The later the period, the more difficult it is to make a clear distinction between what is an indigeneous element and what is foreign. Probably it is more correct to say that the pattern of absorbing foreign influence, to convert it to something essentially Japanese is itself a Japanese tradition. Still, the problem remains which indigenous element in Japan's culture made this cultural adaptation possible. The lack of transcendental values is one of the most important elements in explaining this. In addition, Japan's insular position made it easier for the ruling elite to voluntarily introduce and modify foreign cultures without any fear of creating social tension within the society. Neither Confucianism nor Buddhism are monotheistic, although the latter does have transcendental deities. This may have proven advantageous in avoiding cultural conflict with a Japanese indigenous culture, which also lacked a belief in a single god. Christianity, however, being a monotheistic religion created certain problems as its first introduction into Japan in the sixteenth century clearly revealed. Even today, Japan's Christian population is less than one percent.

Leaving aside the monothesistic aspect, the Japanese people have always been flexible and ready to accept foreign elements whenever these were perceived to be beneficial for the development of the country or the strengthening of the ruling class. Naturally, at times, reaction to the introduction of foreign elements appeared, resulting in necessary modifications of those elements. On the whole, however, the attitude of the Japanese toward foreign culture has been flexible because of their secular state of mind—especially when compared with another secular culture, Confucian China, with its strict orthodoxy maintained by the traditional mandarin examination system. Thus, *because* of Japanese tradition, various Western "isms" have been introduced into modern Japan and have played an important role.

Among these "isms", liberalism was the first to achieve considerable popularity, particularly in the Movement for Freedom and People's Rights (*jiyū minken undō*) in the late 1870s and the early 1880s. But before dealing with the actual development of liberalism in Japan, it is necessary to touch on the problem of translation. The Chinese term *tzuyu* (the same characters are pronounced *jiyu* in Japanese) is usually used to translate "freedom" or "liberty." This Chinese term, however, from ancient times means "self-willed" or "selfish," and in general it has had a pejorative meaning. This naturally created a problem. In 1869, when Yukichi Fukuzawa wrote *Seiyō Jijō* (Situation in the West), which contained a translation of the Declaration of Independence, he had to add a careful note warning the reader not to interpret the term *jiyū* to mean selfishness. He explained that it was because of the lack of an appropriate Japanese term that this word had been used. In China, in order to avoid this misunderstanding, various attempts had been made to replace *tzuyu* with other terms. Why such attempts were not successful has never been satisfactorily explained. One thing is clear, however: in both countries, even given the possibility for misunderstanding, *tzuyu/jiyū* became popular in advocating and encouraging political movements against autocratic rule. It was understood as meaning political emancipation in general.

A similar misunderstanding, which also resulted in encouraging of the Movement for Freedom and People's Rights can be found in Nakamura's translation of Mill's *On Liberty*. Because of the lack of a separate concept of "society" in Japan at that time, Nakamura could not understand the distinction between "society" and "state." In chapter four of *On Liberty*, where Mill talked about society's control over an individual, Nakamura understood it as a problem of the government and the individual. In the same way "collective opinion" was translated "government's opinion." Thus Mill's idea of the "tyranny of the majority" could not be understood by Nakamura, and the simplified dichotomy between the government and the individual became the focal point in the translation.

The term *minken* (people's rights) was also difficult to translate. When it was that the term *ch'üanli* (the same Chinese characters are pronounced *kenri* in Japanese) was first used to translate "right" has not been established. It is clear, however, that the term became popular when it was used in W. A. Martin's translation into Chinese of Henry Wheaton's *Elements of International Law* (Boston, 1863). It was reprinted in Japan in 1865, and was widely read among the ruling elite and the intellectual class. In this case too, *ch'üanli* had the pejorative connotation "weighing profit" in traditional usage in both China and Japan. Various attempts to replace the term failed in both countries. At first, because it appeared in a book on international law, the term *ch'üanli* or *kenri* was used in connection with the rights of a state in international relations and only rarely applied to the rights of individuals.

The term *minken* (people's rights), distinguished from *shiken* (civil rights), was understood as the right of a group of people who were fighting against the Meiji oligarchy rather than the rights of individuals. For instance, a popular slogan, "Expansion of people's rights" at that time meant striving for the increase of political influence of the *minken* movement as a whole. This was the reason Fukuzawa often criticized the movement, saying that the activists in the movement were interested simply in obtaining power and not sensitive to individual human rights and civil liberties. Insofar as "right" is considered to be related to a collectivity rather than individuals, it was not theoretically difficult, and in reality rather common, that the believers in *minken* (people's rights) converted into or fused with the advocates of *kokken* (a state's right *vis-à-vis* foreign powers). The justification for the conversion or fusion was the argument that in order to promote the welfare of the people it was necessary to make the state strong in its competition with Western powers.

In any event, the terms *jiyū* (freedom or liberty) and *minken* (people's rights) were widely used to indicate new principles introduced from the West. In addition to the translation of Mill's works, works by Montesquieu, Rousseau, Spencer, and Bentham were translated and achieved considerable popularity. In 1881 the Liberal Party *(jiyutō)* was formed; interestingly enough its forerunner had been called the Patriotic Party *(Aikokusha)*. Although the Liberal Party survived until 1898, and although, as its official history (1910) declared, its only principle was "liberalism modified by the concept of the state-idea," liberalism actually lost most of its popularity in the late 1880s. Factional conflict within the "liberal" camp in the broadest sense weakened their influence from within. One faction which put emphasis on the idea of liberty was ideologically lead by "an Eastern Rousseau," Chōmin Nakae, the translator of Rousseau's *Social Contract*. Another faction leader was Yukichi Fukuzawa, whose followers were more interested in such practical matters as adopting the British parliamentary system. Both factions worked together when they had the common goal of establishing a popularly elected representative body; however, once the decision was made by the government to introduce a parliamentary system, conflict between factions, rather than cooperation, became the rule.

In the mid 1880s, the Movement for Freedom and People's Rights, mentioned above, was severely suppressed by the government, yet many leaders of the movement were absorbed by the newly established Diet (parliament) when it was established. Because of the movement's strong emphasis on political participation and on obtaining power, once the Constitution of 1889 consolidated the existing régime, many leaders of the movement focused their efforts on becoming influential in party politics. But since the right to vote was limited to the landowner class, many of the rank-and-file participants in the movement, which internally lacked democratic procedures anyway, lost their political importance.

On a more theoretical level, liberal ideas were replaced by the emergence in Japan of a new theory, Social Darwinism. Hiroyuki Katō, who became an advocate of Social Darwinism at the beginning of 1880s, criticized the idea of natural right, which he had previously supported, saying that according to the most recent "scientific" theory the idea of natural right was nothing but an illusion. (To use one Western "ism" to criticize another was to become quite common thereafter.)

Another important result of the Social Darwinist type of thinking was that it increased the Japanese people's feelings of inferiority *vis-à-vis* the great Western powers. This was accompanied by a sense of superiority on the part of the Japanese toward their Asian neighbors, represented by the slogan, "Escape from Asia, enter the West."

Before Japan's consolidation as a modern, unitary nation-state by the promulgation of the Meiji Constitution in 1889, there was still a sympathy and sense of solidarity with both her Asian neighbors and the smaller European nations struggling for independence. For example, when Shirō Shiba wrote a political novel in 1885, he expressed his sympathy with the Irish people. Even among those liberals attracted to the United States as a model, their attention was directed more to the American Revolution than anything else. After Japan's success in establishing a nation-state, however, and particularly after her victory in the Sino-Japanese war, the Japanese tended to limit their interest to the great Western powers, looking down on the smaller, weaker nations of Asia and Europe. In the eyes of the Japanese, these small nations were not successful because they were not adequately equipped for survival; they were not fit.

II

The establishment of a constitutional monarchy and strong central government by the Meiji Constitution, and the subsequent strict censorship, also limited the influence of liberal intellectuals. This was because the question of popular sovereignty ceased to be a question. After the idea of natural right was overtaken by Social Darwinism, it had to be replaced by the theory of the organic state. This was because Social Darwinism could be interpreted so as to allow the replacement of the present ruler by an even stronger one, and therefore did not justify the present ruler retaining power for ever. On the contrary, the organic theory of the state was able to fulfill a more conservative role by justifying the present ruling class as the permanent leaders of the society. This change coincided with the government's imposition of its Prussian-type constitution, together with the adoption of German legal theory. Along with other German legal theories, J. K. Bluntschli's *Allgemeines Staatsrecht* (1852), translated by Hiroyuki Katō and published in Japan in 1870, became very popular, particularly among bureaucrats. The organic theory was in a sense familiar to many Japanese who had a knowledge of Confucianism, because Confucianists considered the social order as an organic unity. In fact, later on, at the beginning of this century, a fusion between Western and Confucian organic ideas emerged among conservative intellectuals.

There was also criticism of the prevailing liberal ideas by advocates of traditional values. It was, however, rather more emotional than theoretical because there was no systematic "ism" rationalizing the traditional values. This lack of a systematic doctrine was also evident in the case of the modern Japanese Empire. Hirobumi Itō, who played a major role in the promulgation of the Meiji Constitution, explicitly stated in the conference on its drafting, "The first thing to be done is to decide the cardinal principle underlying legitimacy." Although he tried to find something equivalent to Christianity in the West, in his view, Buddhism was not influential enough to play such a role, neither was Shintoism, which was also lacking in attractiveness as a religion. Thus he reached the conclusion that, in Japan, only the Imperial family could provide the cardinal principle for national integration. Although the Constitution had, indeed, "constitutional" elements, Article One stated that Japan was to be ruled by an unbroken line of emperors. Although constitutional monarchy was established by the Constitution, constitutional*ism* could not be applied consistently because of the patrimonial basis of the Constitution itself.

The Constitution was followed in 1890 by another important document which further emphasized the patrimonial element: the Imperial Rescript on Education. It was merely a moral code emphasizing an emotional attachment and moral duties to the Emperor. The Rescript carefully avoided any phrases which might be thought to have a religious content. The phrases were also carefully chosen to avoid favoring any particular philosophical school. To a certain extent Confucian ethics were included, but Eifu Motoda's idea of making Confucianism a national morality was not realized in the Rescript. Thus, in supplementing the Constitution, which became the core of the legal system, the Rescript on Education became the cardinal principle of national education and of national morality as a whole. The combination of the two documents represented Imperial orthodoxy but a systematic theology was still lacking. Later one of the ideologues of this orthodoxy stated that the "imperial way" *(kōdō)* should be characterized by this lack of content. In his view, the content could be different at different times in accordance with the changing situation.[1]

This lack of ideological content on the part of the Imperial orthodoxy made it easier to introduce various Western "isms." On the other hand, the imperial orthodoxy could control the thoughts of the nation by means of social pressure. To be criticized for being disloyal to the emperor or not conforming to the orthodox belief in the "national polity," was sufficient grounds to lose one's job or be socially ostracized. Moreover, the lack of concrete content made it difficult for the people to know which "ism" was allowed at what time and to what extent. This was because the standard differed according to the situation.

Generally speaking in the case of Japanese orthodoxy, all seemingly dualistic elements, such as ruler and the ruled, god and man, should be found along a continuous line. Those elements which result in discontinuity should be excluded. The principle of popular sovereignty and transcendental religions fell into this category. With the promulgation of the Constitution, the idea of popular sovereignty was placed outside the realm of public discussion. Then in 1892, two years after the proclamation of the Imperial Rescript on Education, serious disputes took place as to whether Christianity could be reconciled with the principles contained in the rescript.

Dr. Tetsujirō Inoue, a professor of philosophy at the Tokyo Imperial University, attacked Christianity. His major points of criticism were as follows: (1) Christianity does not give priority to the state, (2) it does not emphasize the importance of loyalty to the Emperor, (3) it puts emphasis on the other world rather than on this world, and (4) its teaching of philanthropy means the love of all human beings without any distinction.[2] (This was equivalent to blaming Christianity for being a transcendental religion.) Many Japanese Christians who wished to defend themselves against this attack tended to appease the critics by deemphasizing the transcendental elements in Christianity. They said Christianity was in no way opposed to loyalty to the emperor, and so on. This dispute was called "the conflict between education and religion." The idea was that national education should be based on the Rescript on Education, whereas Christianity was not considered appropriate for national education. One major result of this dispute was an increased control over Christian missionary schools.

National compulsory education developed rapidly and, by the end of the last century, the percentage of those attending school was in excess of ninety percent. It was a historical irony, however, that as a result of this development, many people grew tired and disillusioned with a tightly controlled and ritualized school education based on the rescript. Various reactions occurred, such as widespread political apathy, scepticism and retreatism on the one hand; socialism and anarchism on the other. Quite a few writers showed an interest in the "naturalism" found in French literature and tried to imitate such novelists as Emil Zola. But most of them had, at the same time, a retreatist tendency. What they actually wrote were trivial descriptions of their daily lives or personal experiences, often called "I-novels." After Japan's victory in the Russo-Japanese war in 1905, partly as the reaction to the extreme patriotism during the war, and partly as a result of the relaxation in international tensions, individualistic sentiments revived, particularly among writers, and intellectuals as a whole. However, except for a few writers, such as Sōseki Natsume, who explicitly advocated individualism, few were interested in individualism as a "ism." Their major interest was in the privatized ego rather than the individual in a social context; even so, the suppression of the individual by the rigid controls of the traditional extended family system was indeed the theme of a number of "I-novels."

The above tendency was also related to the development of industrialization and urbanization which inevitably resulted in the atomization of people. Another result of the same development was an increased interest in the "social problem." Rapid unbalanced industrialization had created problems and injustices. Humanists, Christians, and other concerned intellectuals, were aroused by the miserable conditions of the peasants, particularly in an area polluted by a copper mine in Ashio, and the inhumane treatment of workers, particularly in coal mines. Although as early as 1882 there was an Oriental Socialist Party, it was merely a short-lived (one month) group with goals such as "the greatest happiness of the social public" and "equality." As industrialization developed and factory workers increased in number (but were poorly organized), the conditions of factory workers, and of poor people in general, became a "social problem." In 1897 a Social Policy Association emerged among scholars and concerned intellectuals, which attempted to investigate this social problem. It was actually modeled on a German association established in 1873. Its position of opposing both *"laissez faire"* capitalism and socialism was the same as its German counterpart.

Socialist ideas were introduced into Japan from the United States and Germany. In 1898 a Study Group on Socialism emerged; among its members actively committed to socialism a new organization called the Socialist Association was formed in 1900. Then in 1901 a Social Democratic Party was founded as the first socialist party in Japan but it was immediately banned. Of the six founders of the party, all except one, Shūsui Kōtoku, were Christians, two of them having been educated in the United States. It was natural, then, that in the early socialist movement there was a strong Christian influence. At the time of the Russo-Japanese war (1904-1905), a united front anti-war movement was formed between socialists and such nonsocialist Christians as Kanzō Uchimura. After the end of the war, a split occurred between Christian socialists on the one hand and more radical non-Christian socialists on the other. The latter thereafter became the mainstream of Japan's socialist movement.

Later, in 1907, on the occasion of the second annual conference of the Japan Socialist party, there was a serious dispute concerning strategy: whether parliamentary means or direct action should be emphasized. The latter, which was advocated by Kōtoku, was supported by the majority.

Kōtoku was influenced by Henry George and Pyotr Kropotkin among others, but at the same time he had a strong sense of Confucianism. For him socialism "appeared to represent a refinement of the ideals of selfless devotion to society," which was a reflection of his Confucian value, but "strengthened by the weight of modern science and a program for political and economic reform."[3] His proposal for "direct action" was simply the projection of his "pure" idea of selfless devotion to society, yet without having any concrete strategy as to how to organize and radicalize workers. In fact, among socialists at the time it was rather a common phenomenon that they had a strong sense of both the Confucian idea of selfless devotion to society and the *samurai* ethos of self-sacrifice. It was partly because the labor movement at that time was not strong enough to support socialist ideals, and socialists tended to believe that only a selected few could sacrifice themselves to promote the cause of socialism. In 1911 Kōtoku was executed along with eleven others because some of his followers attempted to kill the Emperor. From this time on all kinds of leftist ideas were severely repressed.

III

The death of the forceful and charismatic Emperor Meiji in 1912 left a power vacuum. The new emperor, young and incapable, was manipulated by the surviving Meiji oligarchs. These oligarchs became the target of criticism by a movement to "protect the constitutional system" which emerged immediately after Meiji's death. Political parties, supported by the press and chambers of commerce, lead the movement, and the principle of democracy was emphasized by liberal intellectuals. Sakuzō Yoshino was a leader among such intellectuals. The term coined by him was *mimponshugi* (literally, "the principle of placing emphasis on democracy for the people") rather than *minshushugi* which was used to translate "democracy" but has the implication of "popular sovereignty." The difference had an important political significance. Yoshino, by using the term *mimponshugi*, sought to avoid a discussion of where sovereignty resided. He simply discussed how the existing government system could and should be operated more democratically.

In much the same way as Yoshino, another professor of Tokyo Imperial University, Tatsukichi Minobe, who advocated constitutionalism, became successful in criticizing the autocratic form of government by focusing only on the legal problem in his dispute with his colleague Shinkichi Uesugi, which began in 1912. On the basis of the intensified emotional attachment to the emperor, Uesugi emphasized the emotional and patrimonial aspect of the Imperial rule, minimizing the constitutional element. Minobe tried to maximize the constitutional element by saying that in terms of legal theory, by which he meant German legal theory, such as that of G. Jellineck, the emperor should be considered an organ of the state. Uesugi bitterly criticized Minobe, saying that the latter's theory was disloyal to the Emperor. Minobe, however, carefully limited his argument to the field of constitutional law, by stating that the problem of "national polity" advocated by Uesugi was a matter of national sentiment and hence outside legal theory.[4]

The World War I influenced Japan both economically and intellectually. Economically, World War I stimulated and accelerated industrialization, creating more factory workers. Intellectually, the world trend towards democracy permeated Japan as well. Moreover, a new generation, which lacked a Confucian educational background, was emerging. As a result of the spread of public education, private tutoring by Confucian scholars, which used to play a significant role during the feudal period, ceased to be important. New curricula with a greater emphasis on technical knowledge prevented the children from spending sufficient time on the Confucian classics. For example, Sakae Ōsugi, an anarchist writer, was strongly influenced by Kōtoku but, unlike the latter, had almost no Confucian background. Utilizing his ability in French he translated the works of Kropotkin and Romain

Rolland. Through his writings he became influential among intellectuals and in one sector of workers who believed in anarchosyndicalism. As suggested by the name of his magazine *Modern Thought* which began publishing in 1912, he was considered the champion of modern Western thought, but "modern" is a relative term. The ideas which he was propagating were those which had been widely circulated in the West around the turn of the century, including those of Henri Bergson and Georges Sorel.[5]

Idealism and humanism were other ideas which attained popularity after World War I. The name Tolstoy was often mentioned among intellectuals. To a certain extent, pacifism, such as that of Gandhi, was introduced into Japan (see chapter seven). There was little scope for traditionalists to criticize these tendencies. Only one conservative political leader, Shigenobu Ōkuma, who was the prime minister in 1898, and then again from 1914 to 1916, proposed the idea of "a harmony of Eastern and Western civilizations," placing emphasis on the essential identity between the two. His idea, however, was not influential among intellectuals.

IV

The Russian Revolution of 1917 and the rice riots in Japan in the following year were other epochmaking events. The latter was a series of riots on a widespread scale attacking dealers who withheld rice in anticipation of a price increase. The revolution encouraged leftist and labor movements and the riots resulted in the emergence of a party cabinet, because the surviving oligarchs had to admit that the social disturbances were then out of their control. The movement for the realization of universal suffrage started in 1919 supported by party politicians, intellectuals, the press, and workers. The organized workers influenced by socialist ideology, however, became critical of the movement, pointing out that the movement's goal was simply a bourgeois democracy. Many Marxist documents were translated and distributed and serious conflicts took place between Bolsheviks and Anarchists fighting for control of the labor movement. Although terms such as "social reform" and "social movement" were commonly used, there were disputes concerning strategy as well as ideology. In 1922 the Japan Communist Party was formed underground, but the dispute continued on the definition of orthodox Marxism.

The disputes among Marxists were usually extremely abstract and always full of citations from Marx's works. The method of disputation was similar to that of the Confucianists on the interpretation of the classics, similar also to debates in German jurisprudence. Perhaps both the Confucian tradition and dogmatic German scholarship had some influence here. More importantly, however, the fact that such disputes were carried on among ideological leaders within the Marxist camp who were highly educated but separated from the actual labor movement, resulted in abstract arguments little related to practical strategy.

It is undeniable, however, that Marxism was extremely attractive for many intellectuals as it was their first ideological means to analyze society and to criticize the Emperor system on a theoretical level. This dogmatic system, which was abstract, but in their eyes beautifully structured, appealed to the intellectuals' aesthetic sense. Under the circumstances, the commitment to Marxist ideas carried great risks regarding their future careers, but this was partly a reason for the young intellectuals to throw themselves into the Marxist movement: because of their "pure" (again, aesthetic) passion for self-sacrifice. At times, the fact that one was born into a "bourgeois" family created a sense of guilt, which motivated one to be active in the movement for the emancipation of the proletariat.

A translation of the three volumes of Marx's *Capital* was published between 1920 and 1925, and the complete works of Marx and Engels commenced publication in 1928. Ironically, 1928 was the year the Communists were severely suppressed in the political arena. Thereafter the suppression continued, encompassing eventually even liberals. Marxists, however, were still critical of liberals saying that the latter were ideologues of a bourgeois society. Thus a united front against the trend toward militarism remained impossible.

In the early 1930s liberalism was criticized both by rightists and by leftists for different reasons. The rightists criticized liberalism as being disloyal to the Emperor. Leftists regarded liberalism as something to be overcome along with bourgeois society. Although the reasons were different, those who criticized liberalism shared one common belief that liberalism was the guiding principle of the ruling elites—the senior statesmen, party leaders, business leaders, and bureaucrats. On the other hand, those intellectuals who advocated liberalism felt that liberalism was not really influential at all and merely supported by a handful of people like themselves, who shared the irony of being criticized both from the right and the left.

Of course, the difference in evaluating the influences of liberalism was in part due to the differences in the usage of the term. For those who criticized liberalism, the term was used as a label for the enemy; whereas for those who advocated liberalism, it symbolized a belief in certain institutions that were being threatened. Those who wanted to change the situation, toward either the right or the left, considered liberalism the ideology of the status quo—constitutionalism, parliamentalism, and the party cabinet. On the other hand, the liberals themselves complained about the absence, or the weakness, of such institutions in Japan.

Right wing criticism of liberalism resulted in the denouncement of Minobe's constitutional theory which considered the Emperor as an organ of the state (which had been a legitimate theory for over two decades). Why this happened requires a psychological explanation rather than the analysis of a theoretical dispute. A sense of anxiety had increased because of exacerbated internal difficulties as a consequence of the world economic crisis of 1929. After Japan began her invasion of Manchuria in 1931, a growing international isolation heightened the people's anxiety. Some form of psychological compensation was needed to remedy this anxiety. This was one of the major reasons why a Japanese morality, centered around "national polity," became particularly emphasized. Accumulated resentments among peasants and other underprivileged people who had been sacrificed to rapid industrialization and urbanization, was converted into anti-Western feeling, because Westernism was identified with urbanism. Liberalism was the label for all sorts of defects created by Westernism. Thus "liberals" together with communists ("reds," a term used to mean traitors) became the target of witch-hunting. Minobe was one of the victims. Certain Western ideas such as in Oswald Spengler's *Decline of the West* (vol. 1, 1918 and vol. 2, 1927) and later those of fascism and Nazism were fully utilized to criticize Western liberalism and parliamentarianism.

At least a brief comment is necessary to explain why socialist ideas, which had a predominant influence among intellectuals, not only were not strong enough to check the tendency of the national intellectual climate toward ultranationalism, but also subtly led many Marxists to convert into advocates of ultranationalism. The latter trend cannot be explained by the simple fact of suppression by the government. One common element between socialism and nationalism was collectivism or anti-individualism. Because of this, when socialism was introduced into Japan around the turn of the century, some became "national socialists" who said that socialism was not new in Japan, with its long tradition of collectivist ideas and traditional solidarity (conformity) in rural communities, and the belief that the state (i.e., the emperor) had taken care of the people's welfare.

Of course, the socialists in the 1930s were more sophisticated than the national socialists a generation before, but one of the justifications given for their conversion to ultranationalism was basically the same as that of the national socialists. Another justification was that since both Japan and its Asian neighbors were fighting against Western imperialism (which was buttressed by Western ideology, which included individualism) Japan, as the leader of the Greater East Asian Coprosperity Sphere, should overcome Western civilization by emphasizing the Oriental collectivism common to Asia. Criticism of individualism and liberalism as bourgeois ideologies was an additional element to facilitate this justification. According to some who converted rightward, Asian solidarity, guided by Japan's state-socialism under the emperor, was the most practical way of realizing the socialist idea in Asia. It turned out that this argument was merely a temporary justification of Japanese imperialism. Later, those who argued in this way became supporters of ultranationalism either explicitly or implicitly. The accelerated ultranationalist tendency reached its peak when the slogan "Exterminate the devils: Britain and the USA!" was widely used during World War II.

V

When the Japanese military was defeated by the Allied powers, the Japanese people were forced to concede to the reality of Western superiority. Just as immediately after the Meiji Restoration, the Japanese people again started introducing everything Western, from political ideas and institutions to manners and fashions. Guided by the Occupation authorities, democratization and the shift from feudal to modern attitudes became the most popular tendencies. The United States and Britain now became models Japan should follow.

Since then, nearly all world's "isms" have been introduced into Japan, from existentialism to structuralism, from Maoism to structural reformism. There have been so many that all of them cannot be treated separately. All that can be done here is to indicate some of the characteristics commonly found in the process of their introduction.

It is a common phenomenon in our society, heavily influenced by mass communication media, that one idea (epitomized in a slogan) which is popular for a length of time can easily be replaced by another. For example, during the period of rapid economic growth in the 1960s, a sort of fetishist belief in gross national product prevailed; in the early 1970s social welfare became popular, at least on the surface, although underneath the residue the belief in GNP still remained. Then the oil crisis came, and a "reexamination of social welfare," (i.e., the reduction of expenses for welfare) became the theme. This rapid change in public opinion ought to be called a change of mood rather than a change in "isms." In a mass postindustrial society fragmentation of interests and ideas results in a significant lack of a definite "ism" of any sort, although various "isms" do survive in a pluralistic way in different sectors of society.

In terms of variety there are indeed all sorts of "isms" in the world. Even the new "isms" in the third world have a sort of exotic attractiveness for some Japanese. Those who criticize the present pattern of rapid economic growth tend to seek a new pattern of development in their romanticized image of the third world. But the predominant orientation remains to the West, an orientation which started with the Meiji Restoration and revived after defeat in World War II. Of course, in the thirty-five years since the last war the situation has changed greatly. On the one hand Japan's efforts to "catch up with the West" have been successful, but on the other hand a sense of disillusionment with the West has set in. The war in Vietnam greatly reduced the popularity of the United States. This was exemplified by the fact that in public opinion polls, starting from the mid-1960s, Switzerland (recognized as a peaceful country by the majority of Japanese) replaced the United States as the most preferred foreign nation. The economic conditions in Britain—once the model for the welfare state—and Watergate in the United States, greatly detracted from the idealized image of those countries. Similar to the lack of any dominant "ism," the lack of a foreign state as a model to be followed is a new feature of contemporary Japan.

Against this background, the variety of "isms" introduced into Japan has increased even more, reflecting the people's search for new principles. This is partly because there is now simply more information available. Although this is a new phenomenon, there has been one consistent pattern in that the introduction of "isms" has been compartmentalized. This was the case in early modern Japan when a certain foreign country tended to be most influential in a certain sector of society: The British navy was the model for the Japanese navy, the German army for the Japanese army, and France was considered to be the ideal in literature. This tendency continues even today, with each "ism" introduced into a compartmentalized sector of the society. There is one group of people very enthusiastic about the PLO and there is another that admires the Israeli kibbutz. Each of the groups has detailed information but only through one channel; as a result, there has been no communication among groups, nor even have there been disputes between those groups which are, in some senses, diametrically opposed.

This increased tendency toward diversification of "isms" has resulted in pluralist stagnation rather than in the creativity that could be brought about by communication between the holders of different ideas.

The above situation, to a certain extent, may be a common phenomenon in other highly industrialized countries. In Japan, however, it appears rather extreme because of our historical tradition. First of all, there have been few voluntary associations, or "salons," or such groups as the Bloomsbury Group, for the interchange of ideas. The only exceptions are to be found in the period immediately after the restoration and immediately after the defeat. Whenever a consolidation of the society takes place, compartmentalization increases—which becomes all the more remarkable in Japan because of a strong tendency toward the conformity of the closed in-group (exemplified by the custom of lifetime employment with the same company). Even in the case of scholars, once a career is begun in a certain department or discipline in a certain university, it is normal to stay with that same department or discipline until retirement. With the increase in international communication, this compartmentalization is being weakened to a certain extent, but in another respect such a tendency still continues. For example, a certain school may be interested in introducing a particular set of concepts from abroad and may attempt to monopolize the channels of communication with the other culture.

In any case, the exaggerated situation of compartmentalization in Japan shows clearly that there is a need to develop communication not only across national boundaries but among disciplines and among the different "isms." Today the problem of Westernism and Western "isms" may not be as important as before because Japan is in certain ways already extremely Westernized. However, beneath the surface, continuity does exist, particularly in terms of the pattern of acceptance of the various "isms." For Japan, seeking to establish its own identity in an increasingly complex and at times dangerous world, the problem remains how best to utilize or improve her capacity to absorb new "isms" and even improve some of the older "isms" which to some extent now form an integral part of Japanese culture.

Notes

1. Kenji Maki. *Zōtei Nihonkokutai no Riron,* Yuhikaku, 1944, pp. 132–133.
2. Tetsujirō Inoue, *Kyōiku to Shūkyō no Shōtotsu,* Keigyōsha, 1893, p. 125.
3. F. G. Notehelfer, *Kōtoku Shūsui, Portrait of a Japanese Radical,* Cambridge University Press, 1971, p. 80.
4. For more details about Minobe see, Frank O. Miller, *Minobe Tatsukichi,*

Interpreter of Constitutionalism in Japan, University of California Press, 1965.
5. For more details about Ōsugi see, Thomas Stanley, *Ōsugi Sakae, An Anarchist in Taisho Japan: The Creativity of the Ego,* Harvard University Press (forthcoming).

CHAPTER FIVE

Elements of Tradition and "Renovation" in Japan during the "Era of Fascism"*

Introduction

The aim of this chapter is to shed some light on political developments in Japan during the "era of fascism."[1] The method adopted will be to examine the way in which elements of tradition/"renovation", and those of continuity/discontinuity acted upon each other.[2] Where relevant, certain comparisons between Japan and Germany, which at that time had some common features, will be attempted.

Initially, a brief survey of various Japanese approaches to the study of Japan in the era of fascism will be carried out in order to clarify my own perspective. However, the survey will extend beyond academic studies in the strict sense and will try to describe and analyze the intellectual atmosphere which provided the background to such studies. This is inevitable in that Japanese studies of the era of fascism are not yet fully developed. Japanese scholars have provided a considerable number of studies on specific aspects of the problem but so far, studies that can compare favorably with Karl Bracher's *Die Deutsche Diktatur* are comparatively rare.

The approaches so far adopted in studies of Japanese fascism fall into two paired categories. The first contains two approaches, one which places emphasis on the peculiar nature of Japanese fascism, and one which places emphasis on the universal aspects of Japan's experience. The second paired category also contains two approaches, one which places emphasis on the decade of the thirties being part of a continuous line of historical development, and one which places emphasis on the discontinuity of Japan's historical developments, especially in the thirties. These are the "peculiar/universal" and the "continuity/discontinuity" theses.

Let us first consider those studies on the era of fascism conducted from the end of the war into the fifties. In this period, the "peculiar" approach to Japan's era of fascism was to be found in the writings of the Marxist historians of the so-called *kōza* faction. In order to support their views they emphasised certain features peculiar to Japanese capitalism and the Japanese Emperor system. Other Marxist historians held the "universal" view based in part on the general proposition of Dimitrov's report to the seventh congress of the Comintern: That "a fascism in power is an overt and violent dictatorship by the most reactionary, the most exclusionist and the most imperialistic elements of financial capital." Other, non-Marxist, historians pointed out the feudalistic, i.e. premodern, nature of Japanese militarism.

Early postwar analyses using the "peculiar" approach—seeing either a unique Japanese capitalism or a unique Japanese psychology—were not entirely devoid of the tendency towards generalizing beyond Japan. This was due to the fact that such studies were undertaken with the aim of criticizing the era of fascism in Japan, and thus comparison with the fascism of other nations was necessary. In other words, the differences between these two points of view would appear to be of degree rather than of principle.

As Japan moved into the 1960s, a period of high economic growth, and as the memories of the war faded, a new intellectual climate developed. Views critical of the fascism were no longer able to command the attention of the population. There was an increasingly strong reaction against such criticisms, and there was a revisionist view which attempted to reevaluate militarist Japan in a positive manner. The new situation produced some changes in the two viewpoints mentioned above.

The viewpoint which emphasized the uniqueness of Japanese militarism produced two new trends. On the one hand, there was the nostalgia for militarism represented by the favorable reception accorded Fusao Hayashi's *Daitōa Sensō Kōteiron (An argument in Support of the Greater East Asian War)*. On the other hand, there was the discovery of an indigenous theory of revolution in the writings of Ikki Kita and in the actions of the young officers who took part in the February 26, 1936 rebellion.

These two tendencies, although poles apart in their attitudes towards the system existing in the thirties, do share the emphasis on features peculiar to Japan and evaluate positively aspects of Japanese society during the fascist period. Those who support the arguments put forward in *Dai Tōa Sensō Kōteiron* viewed Japanese history in the era of fascism as the "glory of the Japanese Empire." Those of the left who ironically find the prototype of the romantic revolutionary in the radical rightists of the fascist period, would see such fascism as essentially a revolt against the overall current of the time. In one sense, therefore, the first view is more characteristic of the continuity thesis and the latter is more characteristic of the discontinuity thesis.

It is perhaps appropriate to point out here that the viewpoint emphasising the peculiar nature of Japanese fascism, when combined with a positive evaluation of the era of fascism in Japan, tends to regard phenomena in Japan as unique. This applies whether the evaluation is all-embracing or partial. Such a viewpoint differs considerably from those in the late forties and early fifties who, while placing great stress on the peculiar nature of Japanese fascism, severely criticized it, and therefore retained the potential for generalization. It is true that the postwar period (up to the fifties) did produce emphases on the unique aspects of Japan's national policy from a conservative point of view. They upheld such slogans as "The Emperor, the object of our adoration." In a period when democratization was the order of the day, such views were in a decided minority, but when Japan regained its independence such defensive views (defensive, that is, of the old order) began to gather more support.

The viewpoint which emphasizes the nonuniqueness of what happened to Japan in the 1930s led to an overt tendency to view that era in a positive light. This was due in part to the fact that memories of the war had become less vivid, and in part to the conservative mood nurtured by the nation's prosperity. This new attitude *might* be termed a "modernizationist" view, but it is difficult to reconcile this use of the term with that of S. N. Eisenstadt, who regards fascism as the *breakdown* of modernization.[3] In general, however, it seems reasonable to define this view as one which evaluates the whole process of Japan's rapid development as an example of successful modernization in spite of the fact that Japan was a late-developing country. There are very few academic works in Japan which provide an explicit, positive evaluation of fascism in the manner of R. Dahrendorf on Germany.[4] This is not really surprising, in that this period, for Japan, from a modernizationist perspective, appears to have no special features of its own. Rather, it was simply a part of the linear process of development. Similarly, the tragic experiences of the war are totally ascribable to the special nature of the circumstance called "war."

One can understand this modernizationist approach as one in which the era of fascism is viewed affirmatively, as part of Japan's historical continuity—a view held by those who basically *support* society as it is. However, another viewpoint, one which also emphasizes nonunique-ness and continuity, *opposes* society as it is. Marxists interpret the historical development of modern Japan as one which leads inevitably to "state monopoly capitalism." Although this view is strongly critical of both the present and the past, it seems to confer immunity from responsibility to everyone. This comes from interpreting history as an unbroken chain of inevitabilities. In other words, this particular variant of Marxism, if turned upside down once again, becomes the Hegelian theodicy, "Everything that exists is rational."

Thus far we have examined, albeit briefly, the two pairs of view-points and the four tendencies emergent from them from the end of the war until the 1960s. In appearance, these four tendencies differ radi-cally. Within the views emphasizing the particularist perspective there exists the positive affirmation of the Greater East Asian War, a romanticism resulting from perceiving history as a continuous parade of tradition. Then there is the view held by the New Left who have pursued an indigenous theory of revolution and found in it a rather pathetic identification with the rightist "radicals" in the 1930's. This group however regards history as essentially discontinuous. Among the views emphasizing nonuniqueness or universality one finds: (1) the modernizationist view, with a heavy overlay of the continuity ap-proach; (2) the perspective based upon a theory of "state monopoly capitalism", and this also has aspects of the continuity approach.

Despite their many differences these views have a number of draw-backs in common. In the first place, they all fail to clarify the relation-ship between what is peculiar in history and what is universal. Those who emphasize particularity are so influenced by its evidence that they reject any possibility of generalization. On the other hand, views which focus on universalism have tended to perceive all the twists and turns in the historical process as bearing out some general law. This has resulted in little or no attention being paid to the role played by the individual in history or to the impact of social and cultural factors on historical development.

The second area where deficiencies are evident is that all the views fail to give sufficient consideration to the relationship between the subjective actions of individuals in history and the results such actions bring about. Those subscribing to the argument in the affirmative regarding the Greater East Asian War look at history unquestioningly and romanticize it as a (favorable) natural process. Those in pursuit of an indigenous theory of revolution have succumbed to a pathetic brand of emotionalism, in complete defiance of moral responsibility. "Modernizationists" have reduced history to a set of quantitative conditions and have paid little or no attention to the subjective choices made by individuals. Again, those who adhere to the "theory of state monopoly capitalism" view history as a chain of unbroken inevitabilities and are strongly inclined to a kind of fatalistic determinism.

Although the defects in each view do differ, they are clearly all guilty of neglecting the perspective which considers the relationship between the subjective choices of individuals and their concomitant results. It is precisely this perspective which will receive attention in this essay. The fundamental concern of this essay is to examine those elements of tradition peculiar to Japan as well as those elements of a more universal nature that were observable in the era of fascism. Emphasis will be placed on the similarities as well as the differences in subjective responses to the social situation of that period.

One major problem is to decide what the "social situation" was in this historical period. It might well be called a mass society situation, characterized in the following manner. First, there is a diversification of various organizations and groups all with different interests and conflicting goals. Efforts to achieve a collective assertion of interests through the medium of trade unions and the emergence of a *Parteienstaat* against a background of intense conflict among political parties are typical of this state of affairs. The second phenomenon is political apathy by the masses. This is directly related to the privatization of interests. The third and final characteristic feature of a mass society is an accumulation and intensification of anxiety and discontent, due to a sense of powerlessness and alienation.

The era of fascism in both Germany and Japan did reveal similar trends. There was a strong force for integration at work to check the trend toward diversification. There was considerable political mobilization in order to deal with political apathy. Great efforts were made to channel the anxiety and to divert the discontent by calling attention to real or imagined internal and external enemies. This essay, by keeping in mind the close relationship between traditional and renovationist elements, will attempt to analyze how such responses, which did have certain basically universal features, took on additional features peculiar to Japan.

For the sake of convenience, the era of fascism will be considered at three different levels: ideology or sense of value; organization and leadership; and individual/mass psychology. By putting these together, features peculiar to Japan can then be extracted. These three levels do correspond, approximately, to the three aspects of a mass society described above, however the correspondence is by no means one-to-one, but is a complex of interrelationships.

I. The Era of Fascism Analyzed at the Level of Ideology or Sense of Value

In 1937, the Japanese Ministry of Education, in an attempt to produce an official, unified interpretation of the orthodox ideology compiled and published a booklet *Kokutai no Hongi (The Fundamental Principles of Our National Polity)*. The motivation for the publication is made clear in the introduction, where the authors state, "The confusion, in thought as well as in the social order, which exists today, has forced us to realize the deep need for a proper understanding of the fundamental principles of our national polity." They go on to state that such confusion is not peculiar to Japan.

> All eccentric ideas, such as socialism, anarchism and communism have their roots in individualism, the basis of modern Western thought; as such, these eccentric ideas are simply a manifestation of this basic philosophy in different ways and forms. Recently, however, communism has been found to be unacceptable even in Europe and America where individualism is the basic principle of society. Now they have gone to the extent of throwing off communism, and basic individualism. This can be seen in the rise of totalitarianism and nationalism, or in the rise of fascism and nazism. In other words, individualism has been found to be bankrupt and is throwing both the West and Japan into a similar state of confusion in social thought and social order. This development is drawing both Japan and the West to a turning point.

What is made clear in the above is that Japan and the West shared a need to cope with the existing state of "confusion." But, immediately after this observation, there is a sudden move away from a discussion of similarities in problems faced, and the authors begin to maintain that a correct understanding of the "fundamental principles of our national polity" can have only one solution in the Japanese case: "The problems of the Japanese people today, the constant wavering in the midst of different thoughts, restlessness and cultural confusion can only be solved when we Japanese reach a full understanding of the fundamental principles of our national polity, while at the same time discerning the true nature of Western thought."

What is the underlying logic which binds a recognition of the universality of problems in this historical period with an insistence that the solution to such problems can only be found by adopting a particularistic approach? In order to answer this, one has first to consider what aspects of Nazi ideology were incorporated within the orthodox Japanese ideology, then how such aspects were modified to suit the Japanese situation.

Here, one must take up the important theme of *Gemeinschaftsidee* which functioned as an ideology of integration to stem the tendency towards diversification. Members of the *Showa Kenkyukai* (Showa [the "public" name of Emperor Hirohito] Study Group), the "brain trust" of Prince Konoe, all shared a common community or cooperationist view. As one member pointed out, "Planning and control became extremely important. It became necessary to carry out all inclusive national mobilization in a somewhat similar way to that cooperation which exists between capital and labor. . . . Prior to that [National Mobilization] the idea of *ikkun banmin* [one sovereign reigning over all the people as equals] was propagated from rightist quarters. After that, as the China Incident expanded, it became impossible to retain control of the situation. After all, the cooperationist view, the doctrine of the East Asian Community and the like were rather more necessities of state policies with only a coating of thoughts rather than well defined bodies of ideas in themselves."[5]

The Japanese doctrine of community was created to meet the needs of state policies but it was not without its merits. As that same member of the Konoe "brain trust" recollected, it was regarded as "a point of congruity where those leaning toward extreme patriotism, those with a nationalist view and even those with some leaning towards socialism could agree. On the basis of this, Japan could thus join hands with Asia."

Naturally, a doctrine of community formulated to bring together traditional and extreme right wing patriots inevitably differed from the idea of *Volksgemeinschaft* advocated by the Nazi regime. Despite such differences, the Japanese and German doctrines of community had at least one thing in common: they were both used as instruments in efforts to stem the tide of liberalism, individualism, and democracy and as instruments for overcoming the trend towards diversification resulting from these ideas.

A book by Yoshihiko Taniguchi, *Theory of the New Order* (1940) is full of remarks reminiscent of Nazi ideology. For example, he maintained that "the basic idea of the New Order is characterized by its emphasis on integration rather than individualism, on centralized control as against liberalism and on the principle of leadership as against the principle of democracy." But he hastens to add that this principle is "akin to the traditional way of thinking in Japan, which is in accord with the unique characteristics of Japan." Also, he points out that the idea of "the New Order" and the traditional way of looking at the *ie* (household) and its enlarged form, the state, fundamentally are in complete agreement with each other on certain points.[6]

In Germany, the idea of *Volksgemeinschaft* had to be created on the basis of the "mythology of the twentieth century." Japan, on the other hand, being extremely homogeneous racially, linguistically, and religiously, had no need to resort to this. In Japan where all of the 8 million gods and goddesses of heaven and earth were believed to have been in harmonious existence from ancient times, conflict for ascendency among different views of the world (or among potentially jealous gods) never developed. The tendency toward a diversification characteristic of mass society could both develop and be contained within the framework of the emperor system. This became apparent after the communists, who had dared to directly challenge the orthodox ideology of the emperor system, were silenced by a thoroughgoing series of repressive measures from March 1928 until the "group conversions" of 1933. This conversion, or recantation, was rationalized on the grounds that "objectively speaking" Japanese workers were in support of the emperor system. Thereafter, all ideological conflict was reduced to matters of relative emphasis, all carried out within the confines of the emperor system.

This relativization of conflict found its ideological expression in arguments denouncing views which laid stress on absolute or irreconcilable conflicts. Kishio Satomi, in his *Epistemology for the National Polity* stated as follows: "The way of looking at god, nature, and man as antagonistic toward each other has its origin in the Old Testament. So long as one subscribes to this view and regards man and god as opposing each other, it is impossible to understand the peculiarly Japanese concept of the emperor." Equally undesirable was the view which regarded the relationship of ruler and ruled as one of antagonism: "It is clear, from mythology, history and the study of Japanese thought, that the relationship between the Japanese emperor and the Japanese people is one of unity between ruler and ruled . . . . both are united, not as a result of compromise, but genuinely in their respective functions and responsibilities."[7]

Thus, having forcibly removed the most unyielding elements, having managed at the level of ideology to confine the concept of conflict to the realm of relativity, supporters of the orthodox ideology, the establishment, actively set about propagating such slogans as "Showa Restoration" and "One sovereign reigning over all the people as equals," and managed to bring even the proponents of reform under its control.

It would perhaps be useful to pause here and consider why it was possible for the orthodox emperor system ideology to control the various elements of opposition. According to a book on *The Theory of the National Polity* written by Kenji Maki in 1944, the *kōdō* (imperial way) "is supposed to change as the situation requires" and therefore "one of its fundamental characteristics is, that its concrete political goals are, in a manner of speaking, empty."[8] This, of course, meant that the "empty" room could be filled with anything at all, provided that such elements were not characterized by mutual antagonism.

Such being the case, what were the elements utilized to fill this "empty" room, in order to cope with the "necessary situation"? At a press conference, just prior to the inauguration of the *Taisei Yoku-sankai* (Imperial Rule Assistance Association), 1940, Premier Konoe explained the Association's characteristics in the following way:

> There are some criticisms that the New Order Movement has, as one of its undercurrents, communist ideology. I would not deny that some "converts" are active in the movement. We sometimes make use of their knowledge and accept suggestions from them. However, the basic purpose of this movement is to clarify the concept of our national polity. The New Order is like a huge drum; if you pound it hard, it reverberates loudly; if you hit it gently, it reverberates gently. Sometimes it may be resonant with Nazism and sometimes with communism. But the New Order should be deeply rooted in our national polity and its actions should conform to the true way of a loyal subject.

There were many who had had great hopes for Konoe and consequently there were also a great number of criticisms. On this occasion, the inauguration of the Imperial Rule Assistance Association, he found himself utterly incapable of issuing any meaningful declaration or program. All he could say was, "The program of this movement is summed up in the following phrases: 'Assistance to the Imperial rule' and 'Fulfillment of our duties as loyal subjects.' Apart from this, there is no program, no declaration." It may well be that the metaphor of the "drum" was conceived at this time when Konoe was in considerable difficulties with preparations for the establishment of the I.R.A.A. In any case, the metaphor eloquently suggested what actually filled the "empty" place wherein the political goals of the Association were contained.

If, by reference to the history of thought, we look at how the ideologies of left and right were incorporated into the "renovationist" New Order movement, then the following summary is the result. During the process where, as described previously, the left wing became "Japanized," revolutionary left wing thought gradually changed into an ideology of "nationalist renovation." Left wing intellectuals, having been deprived of the chance of achieving revolution by means of mass organizations, and having "converted" from communism, now came to hold the view that they would be able to spread leftist ideology throughout the system by approaching the center of political power and securing a position in it. Renovation, for these people, was the only effective substitute for revolution. Actually, a considerable number of such people moved in this direction with a "revolutionary" passion. Such ex-Communists attempted to justify their stance ideologically, on the grounds that "renovation" was a means of going beyond the existing capitalist system by criticizing it. In that sense, they believed, it had certain elements in common with socialism.

One important channel, through which converted left-wingers were absorbed by the state machinery, did exist. That channel was the movement toward a military state, a policy advocated most insistently by the military themselves. Such a policy was based not on ideology but on a policy which called for technocrats trained in the areas of mapping out "comprehensive plans."[9] Many leftist (or renovationist) intellectuals, who dreamed of controlling the state machinery, were employed to carry out work in this area. These intellectuals, switching from revolutionary movements to renovationist movements, changed from movement activists to state technocrat/administrators. Indeed, the "controlled state" brought into existence by the need to deal with the situation during the era of fascism was in desperate need of professional knowledge and skills both for the creation of comprehensive plans and for putting those plans into effect.

In the case of right wing extremists who took part in the New Order Movement, their attitudes differed from those of Japan's traditional right wingers. In a book with the astonishing title, *The Emperor and the Proletariat* (1929) Kishio Satomi advocated the need for starting a "turbulent movement to unite all the proletarians, courageously, guided by the great cause embodied in our national polity." According to Satomi, the emperor was not a ruler distinct from the ruled; he (the emperor) is supposed to subject himself to the idea of the national polity whose goal is to raise the welfare standards of the proletariat as a whole. "In Japan, it is not the emperor but the national polity that should be accorded the highest esteem. . . .Even the emperor ought to deign to bow before the national polity—this should be the way." This being the case, "it should be extremely clear whether we ought to side with Marx or work with the Emperor in striving for the grandiose undertaking of radical social reform within Japan."[10] Such an undertaking aimed at realizing the "national polity which is designed to improve the welfare of the whole nation." What is presented here is a "renovationist rightist" attempting to propagate the "principle of national polity" among the proletariat by utilizing leftist political rhetoric.

Satomi's view, one has to add, was rather exceptional within the right wing camp. This was in part due to the date of publication, 1929, several years before the movement toward control of all aspects of society reached its peak, a movement Satomi's thesis actually helped to promote. By the latter half of the 1930s, control had reached such a high level that the word "proletariat" itself became taboo, to say nothing of mentioning "proletariat" in the same breath with "emperor." In this sense, Satomi's work is best viewed as the product of a transitional period, transitional in the sense that those on the right, in their efforts to "destroy the status quo" directed a frontal attack on Japan's ruling elite, such as the "liberal" elder statesmen, senior advisers, political parties, and those whom they saw as monopolizing the economic sphere. They also tried at the same time to incorporate populist elements by utilizing such slogans as *"ikkun banmin."* When this "renovationist" movement produced the Imperial Rule Assistance Association and when the high powered military state intensified control and regulation, the role and power of such nongovernmental right wing elements declined significantly. This did not mean that their doctrine of the national polity lost its role entirely at this stage. The ideology of the Japanese Empire remained intact, until the very end, a view of Japan as both a controlled state and a moral state.

To be sure, Japanese ideology in the era of fascism did have one new feature not previously seen, that is, the emphasis on technical control. But this should not be taken to mean that the traditional sense of value was replaced. To cite one example, Taniguchi, in his *Theory of the New Order,* despite stressing the importance of technical control, maintained that "the idea of the New Political Order is also characterised by its emphasis on moralism as against authoritarianism, and on the principle of rule by virtue as against legalism." Now, emphasis on moral aspects and emphasis on rational control and efficiency are basically incompatible with each other. Interestingly, there did exist, within the Association for Service to the State through Industry, a productivity faction and a right-idealist faction, led by Kazuo Ōkochi and Haruo Naniwada, respectively. These factions were in conflict as to which of the two aspects ought to be given the greater weight. But in spite of such conflicts, both explicit and implicit, Japanese ideology in the era of fascism somehow managed to keep placing emphasis on both of them. To understand this state of affairs, one must bear in mind that a forcible display of state power as a means of strictly controlling people within Japan was referred to (i.e., rationalized) as the "whip of love." By the same token, as Japan began its violent career overseas the invasion of China was rationalized, in the words of General Iwane Matsui (commander-in-chief of the Japanese Expeditionary Forces at Shanghai), as a fight between brothers and a "method of urging self-reflection by the elder brother (Japan) because he loved his younger brother (China) too much."

II. The Era of Fascism Analyzed at the Level of Organization and Leadership

Masami Sugihara, author of *Political Power of the National Organization*, stated in 1940, immediately before the inauguration of the Imperial Rule Assistance Association, his summary of the historical background to the national organization then called the New Order as follows:

> The proletarian movement in Japan, which came into existence 20 years ago, and the renovationist (rightist) movement which made its start, explosively, in the wake of the May 15th incident 10 years ago, though crude in their respective methods and ideas, have gradually come to form waves and currents running in one direction. These movements, though initially commencing from their own perspectives, have converged over the issue of one national organization. Needless to say, external factors have also played a strong role in influencing the issue. The net result of all this is what we now have today, namely, the issue of a national organisation which appears under the guise of an issue concerning the New Order.[11]

This asserts that the proletarian movement and the renovationist movement—especially in the latter's relationship to the May 15, 1932 "incident" when rightists assassinated Premier Inukai—together form the essential background to the New Order movement, strikes some people as very strange today. It nevertheless remains true that, from the 1920s, both leftist and rightist groups energetically made attempts to inculcate interests and feelings (especially patriotic feelings) among the masses. Such activities were not limited to groups on the left, such as the labor and peasant unions. Members of reservist and young men's associations formed the overwhelming majority of the 30,000 people mobilized for the National Foundation Ceremony in 1936, the first mass demonstration of its kind organized by the right wing. Members of the reservist associations, in particular, played a major role in such mass organizations. This is shown clearly in Ikki Kita's *Nihon Kaizo Hoan Taiko (General Outline of Measures for the Reconstruction of Japan,* 1931). He pinned great hopes on the reservist members as important agents for that reconstruction. Reservists were to play an important role in the movement for the clarification of the national polity which occurred in 1935 in the wake of the so-called "organ theory controversy." This theory postulated that the Emperor was an organ of the state, albeit the supreme one. This implied that the Emperor, while superior to all others, was yet subservient, like all others, to the state. The National Convention of Associations of Reservists attempted to organize the strong antipathy of the masses towards intellectuals and the elite and to direct these feelings towards ultranationalism; they adopted, on August 7, 1935, a resolution calling for its three million members to join hands and "strive for the clarification of the national polity."

In the fascist period, the right wing activists outside the government, who had hitherto emphasized the importance of national polity only at the level of ideology, now began to compete with the leftists in engaging actively in the organization of the masses. The All Japan Patriots Joint Struggle Council, known as *Nikkyo,* was formed in 1931, its objective being the creation of a united front. It defined itself as an "orthodox revolutionary struggle corps" dedicated to the advancement of a "patriotic movement of the masses" and a "patriotic movement of the proletariat" and issued an emotion-filled appeal, "Let's carry the flag of *Nikkyo* into the villages and into the factories. Let's lay the foundations for a mass struggle and form a movement of militant cells and branches."

One Army pamphlet aroused much public discussion. The document, *Kokubō no Hongi to Sono Kyōka no Teishō (Fundamental Principles of National Defense and Proposals for its Reinforcement,* 1934) also underlined the importance of organizing efforts toward national mobilization on the grounds that "since modern war is a contest between *organized capabilities,*" (original emphasis) it was "absolutely necessary to organize and control as one indivisible entity all elements connected with national defense."

Since the 1920s, efforts in the direction of creating mass organizations, made by those on the left, on the right, and by the military, came to coalesce during and following the Great Depression. This depression hit the countryside hardest and the coalescence of forces formed one large current ushering in the renovationist national movement. In agriculture, tenancy disputes continued to be the target of repeated repression. Nevertheless, the grave damage inflicted by the agricultural crisis produced peasant movements on an increasingly larger scale. For example, the Special Police Division took note of the new trend in its 1932 report on newly emergent tendencies. It noted where "committees to cope with the situation, hitherto composed only of men of influence in the local community, such as town and village headmen, chairmen of the local agricultural associations, and the like, are now being gradually replaced by various forms of mass movements such as mass meetings of villagers, residents of districts, or peasants." It also noted yet another phenomenon where "a certain date is set aside as a petition day and a prefecture-wide petition campaign is carried out." One report stated that a petition campaign for the relief of villagers, organized by the *Jichi Nomin Kyōkai* (Association for Peasant Self-Government) managed to collect some 32,000 signatures.

In response to the emergence of such mass movements, the Government launched a Movement for the Economic Regeneration of Agricultural, Mountain, and Fishing Villages. The aim was clearly the reorganization of the social order in these village communities. In this connection, extremely important was the government-initiated Five Year Plan for the Expansion of Industrial (Agricultural) Associations. This plan, by a revision of the Industrial (Agricultural) Association Law, aimed at the incorporation of "each and every tiller" into Industrial Associations. Such associations had four principal functions: supply of credits, purchasing services, sales, and administration of utilities. They were planned as a means of controlling every aspect of a peasant's daily life, and even a magazine, *Ie no Hikari (Light of the Household)* was published as a means of controlling the peasant mind. This magazine eventually had a circulation exceeding one million.

Left wing activists, denied the opportunity, due to constant repression, of participating in a radical peasant movement, found a legal substitute in the Movement for Economic Regenerations especially in organizations such as the *Sangyō Kumiai Seinen Renmei* (The Industrial Association Young Men's League). In addition a considerable number became active in the *Yokusan Sōnendan* (Imperial Rule Assistance Young Adults Corps).

Similar efforts at organization were directed towards industrial workers, no doubt facilitated by the vacuum left due to government repression of the left wing and revolutionary labor movements. These efforts were principally focused on the *Sangyō Hōkoku Undō* (Service to the State through Industry) a movement aimed at creating "an organization with, as its basis, an all-encompassing organization of employees of every enterprise." In other words, an enterprise community in which the "principle of the enterprise as one body is to be the guiding spirit." This movement managed to incorporate right wing social democrats, converted leftists, and national socialists. However, in spite of its proclaimed goal, "a movement to organize the nation as a whole through the joint efforts of the state and the people," it was, by nature, a government front: a movement for "renovation from above."

These efforts, in various areas and in various forms, formed the essential elements from which the New Order was launched in 1940. This renovationist movement, after inauguration, appeared to have successfully achieved an integration of all the previous efforts at organizing the masses. Masami Sugihara stated as follows:

> When the proletarian movement started, it was anticapitalist based on feelings of hatred and rejection towards capitalists. Now it has succeeded in raising itself to the level where it can criticise the capitalist order from a sense of contributing towards the development of the Japanese nation as a whole. The renovationists on the right commenced their activities as a result of their recognition of the fact that the national polity was on the very brink of a crisis and out of hatred of activists in social movements whom they regarded as traitors. Today, they are establishing themselves as powerful critics engaged in criticising the capitalist and liberal order for the interest and development of Japan as a whole. . . . Today, the differences between leftists and rightists are scarcely discernible. They are becoming human resources of a similar hue.[12]

To be sure, this statement reflects a considerable amount of wishful thinking on the part of Sugihara. There had certainly been a considerable intermingling of left and right elements and this had been proceeding at a considerable pace. Even the police had sounded a warning on this aspect: "As it is often said, the line between left and right is very thin and it is indeed difficult at times to distinguish one from the other."[13] Nevertheless, it certainly did not mean that there was an actual unification of left and right.

In fact, the New Order movement was emasculated as a result of conflicts among the various elements incorporated within it. Although originally designed to "regard the existing political parties as enemies, reject bureaucratic government and organize the masses under a political leadership with a unique national character," the movement signally failed to achieve anything really significant other than the creation of The Imperial Rule Assistance Association. Even that was no great achievement, as it failed to achieve recognition as a political organization and instead simply functioned as a government-manufactured public organization, a supplementary organ of the government, funded totally by the government and staffed primarily by bureaucrats.

However, despite its excessive subordination to the government, the Imperial Rule Assistance Movement did achieve one thing of note. It managed to create all-encompassing organizations in all areas of the country and brought them all under one umbrella organization. But this system suffered badly from a distinct lack of coordination and adjustment among its component parts. The most important development was the result of a cabinet meeting on August 14, 1942, when it was decided to incorporate all village and town block associations throughout the country under the Imperial Rule Assistance Association. Reporting on this, the bulletin of the association, issue 83, boasted: "The 100,000,000 member national organization has now been formed!" Prior to this, local self-governing bodies had consciously avoided interfering too deeply into the realms of private life. But now, village and town associations ceased to be friendship associations, as they formerly had been, and began to meddle actively in the private lives of residents, acting as agents of the municipal governments.

It should be noted here that this 100 million member national organization was certainly not a monolithic one brought into existence under the leadership of one political party after having totally destroyed the organizations already in existence. The town and village block associations modeled on the five-family neighborhood unit of the Tokugawa feudal period, retained and utilized a sense of solidarity which already existed. Also, the IRAA remolded this solidarity to suit a particular purpose. In the case of the various trades organizations a considerable effort was made to take the greatest possible advantage of both the existing organization and the sense of solidarity existing in Japanese enterprises. The latter was of course an embodiment of the view that the employer and the employees of an enterprise formed one family.

The principle of leadership *(Führerprinzip)* coined by the Nazis was often positively referred to in Japan. However, it was interpreted as *shūgi tōsai* (centralized control over public discussion). Moreover, this principle of centralized control was regarded as the antithesis of the principle of majority rule. It was also considered to be identical with the principle of harmonious consensus which had its roots deep in Japan's history and tradition and has been kept alive in village communities. Symbolically, the Imperial Rule Assistance Association Central Committee was called *Kokumin Sōjōkai* (The People's Grand Regular Meeting), suggesting a national version of the block association's *jōkai* (regular meeting).

Sometimes, the principle of leadership was understood to mean that "decisions by the elites or executives are not something reached on the basis of majority rule by mutually chosen representatives as is the case in democracy. Rather such decisions are reached by those people who have been selected by their superiors." In fact, a government-appointed prefectural governor served as chairman of the prefectural branches of the Imperial Rule Assistance Association. Even the Young Adult Corps of that same organization, originally supposed to be a "comradeship organization of the elite" had, at the very top, a prefectural governor, the chairman of the prefectural branch of the IRAA. As the leader-emeritus, he appointed the leader and the vice-leader.

Although the "national" aspect of the "national movement" was accompanied by a great fanfare, the movement was, in reality, nothing more than a forcible integration of the masses into a "high-powered" military state or a controlled state under the direction of renovation-oriented bureaucrats. Indeed, once the movement had got under way, even renovationist groups outside of the government were also forcibly integrated. These nongovernment groups were simply used to get the movement under way. Once that had been achieved, the movement came to be dominated by bureaucrats and those groups that had managed to maintain close affiliations with the bureaucratic machine.

The Dainihon Seinento (The Greater Japan Young Man's Party) which, with its uniform, bore the closest resemblance to the Nazi party, proclaimed that it would achieve a membership of 100,000 by 1940. However, it was compelled to assert that its "organizing activities" were designed to "strengthen the unity within towns and village" and to "take the lead in bringing village (and town) block associations and various other groups into harmonious unity." In the end, all such nationalist groups were unsuccessful in their attempts to mobilize the masses. They had to be content with either continuing their activities on a reduced scale from their drill halls or private schools or to try to strengthen their ties with influential political or bureaucratic figures.

Under the Imperial Rule Assistance Movement, which had been created from a myriad of existing groups and organizations, reference to the principle of leadership did not, as was the case in Germany, imply that authority must reside in one leader. The rejection of a separation of ruler and ruled at the ideological level existed also at the organizational and leadership levels. One basic feature of the system was that authority was delegated in a seemingly endless chain. If one deletes the term "endless" then it is almost identical with bureaucratic control and in fact, bureaucratic control formed the central core of the system. The principal difference is that, within the IRA system, authority extended upwards and downwards. In the upward direction, authority was sought in an endless chain extending far back into history and to the imperial ancestors. In this context, one should recall the words of Satomi: "In Japan, it is not the emperor but the national polity that should be placed in the highest esteem."[14] In the downward direction, authority trickled down until it vanished, like mist, in village communities at the very lowest level. A system of authority naturally corresponds with a system of responsibility but clearly, in this particular case, responsibility could be shuffled easily, either upward or downward, resulting in a system of irresponsibility. Japan, therefore, although it had a principle of leadership, did not have a führer, and when the 100 million member organization was completed, each member became a kind of leader in his or her own right. The natural consequence of such shared responsibility was the so-called *ichioku sōzange* ("repentance of 100 million") whereby the 100 million Japanese, together, at the same time, repented at the end of the war and sought to erase their guilt for the crimes committed.

III. The Era of Fascism Analyzed at the Level of Individual and Mass Psychology

Germany, as a result of defeat in World War I, the revolution, hyperinflation and the severe antagonism between parties on the left and right, experienced in societal terms, a form of acute *anomie*. The crisis which Japan experienced in that same period seemed far more moderate in both scope and depth. But, after all, a sense of crisis is a matter of perception and not measurable by the extent of the objective situation. This is especially true in the case of Japan. It was thought, for example, that a "dangerous thought" of foreign origin, could become contagious in a highly homogeneous and tightly woven society.[15] If such a thought took root, it was feared that it would become endemic throughout the nation. But the feared disruption of the harmony existing in society came, rather, from the psychological impact of rapid and uneven urbanization.

Urbanization, from the point of view of influence on the individual, probably means their emancipation from the traditional communal life in a rural community. At the same time, it also means that an individual's relationship with other members of society becomes more impersonalized, that he is detached from the protection of primary groups to which he belongs and therefore, the individual is made to feel more helpless and isolated than before.[16]

Japan's rapid and artificial process of industrialization, under the slogan of *Shokusan Kōgyō* (Increase Production and Promote Industry), in order to achieve national prosperity and a strong military, was accompanied by urbanization which provided, not emancipation, but a growing sense of isolation and helplessness. Those who were forced to leave or chose to leave, the countryside to join the urban workforce, invariably did so without adequate psychological preparation. City life lacked a supportive community environment which made the new urban workforce feel even more isolated and helpless. It was perhaps natural that the solution, in the case of these immigrants was to turn, when desperate, to the countryside for support. Thus a system of "working away from home" with a guaranteed place in the countryside to return to was rather more common than a system where workers were completely self-reliant.

The agricultural crisis of the 1930s effectively destroyed even this refuge for the urban workers and thus their sense of anxiety was greatly increased. The intensified anxiety became entangled with a view of ascribing Japan's crisis to urbanization. Urbanization, in turn, was regarded as identical with Westernization. The result was that the anxiety was channeled into an antiurban elite, an anti-intellectual, anti-Western ultranationalism. In the process, the ideology of Japanese fascism began to take on a strong agrarian flavor.

The government response to the agricultural crisis was, as stated previously, to launch a "Movement for Economic Regeneration." This policy, from a psychological perspective, was an attempt to cope with the feelings of anxiety by converting them into a springboard that would nurture a strong sense of dependence among the populace. The *Japan Agriculture News,* the official organ of the Japan Agricultural Association, made the point clearly in its editorial of June 28, 1937:

> In order to guide poor peasants who are seriously lacking in the areas of independence and autonomy, the policy should be to *place their feelings of dependence on a better and more stable basis.* To be more precise, the policy should be to help these people maintain their livelihood by neighbourhood cooperation. In order to carry out this policy, they should be brought more deeply into the village blocks, that is, communal groups which have traditionally served as the basis of agrarian social life, and into the communal units of agricultural associations, the institutionalized variants of the above communal groups.

Similarly, in urban areas, the concept of the "enterprise as one family" was emphasized in order to induce workers to become more dependent on their companies; these companies functioning as pseudo-primary groups, could then be utilized to eliminate the anxiety experienced by the urban workforce. The rural depression also affected the urban workforce in that those employees who were "working away from home" were conscious of the deterioration in the very areas they wished to return to in times of need. The "enterprise as one family" concept was indeed also intended to wean workers away from this dependence on their rural places of origin by turning the enterprise into a pseudo-community. A lifetime employment system and a paternalistic management system provided the material basis for such an ideology.

The efforts made, not only with reference to the rural and urban workers but also in all other areas, were all intended to transform anxiety into a sense of increased dependence. It is, of course, true that certain groups incorporated into the overall national organization were rather half-hearted in their support. One classic example was the *Bungaku Hōkokukai* (Association for Service to the State through Literature) which considered creating, within its own organization, a means of protecting the autonomy of works of literature. Still others within that organization wished for incorporation simply for convenience. What is really important here is that, regardless of whether the participation of groups in the national organization were undertaken with conviction or simply for convenience, it was inevitable that all should take part in the imperial rule system. Once an individual participated, even passively, some of the values of the umbrella organization would inevitably be inculcated into that same individual.

It would be innaccurate, however, to state that the anxiety which permeated Japanese society in the era of fascism was completely absorbed by this institutionalization of a sense of dependency. The fact that such anxiety did at times find outlets in destructive actions ought not to be overlooked. In this respect, it may be useful to note the differences between Japan and Germany. In Germany, the destructiveness which emerged from the discontented social elements was an important factor in the rise of Nazism, and the root of destructiveness was to be found in the "isolation of the individual and suppression of individual expansiveness."[17] In Japan, in contrast, the anxiety was often manifested as a threat to an individual's vested interests in the old system. Admittedly, such vested interests were usually rather insignificant, e.g., small plots of land owned by so-called "owner-cultivators of medium standing" or "farmers of the empire." The transformation of the anxiety into a heightened sense of dependence was used as the catalyst, and an artificial sense of crisis from without was created. One must keep these fundamental differences in mind when examining the Japanese history of destructive action emanating from that intensified anxiety.

In Japan, as in Germany, those who advocated "reform" because of its potential for destroying the existing *status quo,* were either people living in obscurity or were those who regarded themselves as representatives of such people. However, in Japan, those who "represented" obscure or marginal people vastly outnumbered the actual marginal people among the activists. For example, the young military officers of the *putsch* were all graduates of cadet schools; Ikki Kita, although he did not complete middle school, came from a reputable family in Nigata prefecture (in any case, the number of people graduating from middle school at this time was rather small); Shumei Ōkawa was a graduate of Tokyo Imperial University. In the German case, marginal men were the leaders of the German Nazi movement. Adolph Hitler was an ex-lance corporal whose father was the illegitimate son of a housemaid.

Moreover, the leaders of the Nazi party were marginal not only in terms of class origins but also geographically. Hitler was born in Braunau, Austria; Alfred Rosenberg was born in Riga, Latvia (now in the Soviet Union); Rudolph Hess in Egypt, and Richard Walther Darre in Argentina. Kita was born on an isolated island, Sado, but it is peripheral only within a small and extremely homogeneous country. The bureaucrats who had spent many years in Manchuria before playing an active role in the renovationist movement might be regarded by some as geographically marginal but, in fact, they were dispatched to that country because they were the cream of Japanese bureaucrats at that time. They returned home to Japan having gained great experience in applying renovationist policies in a Japanese controlled area.

In the February 26, 1936 "incident"—a violent *putsch* by junior officers involving the assassination of a number of high officials—anxiety and discontentment exploded in a most destructive manner. This attack upon the higher by the lower was in no way intended to destroy the hierarchical system of authority. Rather, it was intended to "clear the court of corrupt elements." The young officers rejoiced when an official announcement was made by the minister for the army that the "motives of the uprising have reached the emperor's ears." But in the end the officers were regarded as rebels and punished.

The rebellion of these young officers clearly reflected their sense of crisis. The principle of the national polity which was their reference point in justifying their action was no longer the same as that advocated in the late Meiji period (the beginning of this century). At that time, the national polity was viewed as static, a continuous neatly arranged hierarchical system with families at the bottom, prefectures in the middle, and the state at the top, all in perfect harmony with each other. The young officers' concept of the national polity was a projection of their anxiety and discontent which found explicit expression in their demands for radical change. In spite of this, their insurrection must be regarded as "dependent insubordination" in that they wished to render powerless the existing intermediate functionaries, not the system as a whole.

Takeo Doi has neatly described one very important feature of Japanese society, the concept of *amae* whereby one presumes upon another's generosity or behaves like a spoiled child.[18] A person who holds this *amae* toward another often displays a stubborn resistance and assumes a spiteful attitude toward that other and it appears as if he is rebelling against that person. In fact, this sort of behavior is not insubordination; the *amae* is simply a means of drawing attention from, and receiving greater protection from, the other. This sort of pseudo-rebellious behavior is best labelled "dependent insubordination." The behavior of the young officers is a case in point. If *amae* is in essence a craving for psychological identification with a certain object, then dependent insubordination as one manifestation of this *amae* induces the "rebels" to feel that their objectives will be fulfilled as soon as the object of their *amae* shows understanding of their motives. This is clearly seen in the young officers' attitude toward the emperor.

Thus, a seemingly destructive manifestation of anxiety and discontent, incapable of being transferred directly into an institutionalised sense of dependence, manifested itself as an insubordination confined within the framework of *amae*. In this way, it indirectly contributes to the institutionalization of that dependence.

Ironically, the rebels who sought to destroy or alter the intermediary forces of the controlled bureaucratic state and to identify themselves more closely with the emperor and the national polity, actually aided—indeed accelerated—the development of the very system they were trying to destroy. The result of their effort was in fact an intensification of control within the controlled state aided by the free use of sophisticated technology. The execution of the rebels eliminated the possibility of another mutiny and at the same time gave the military authorities an even greater say in political affairs. Japan was pushed even further and faster along the road to a military state. As the institutionalization of dependence permeated throughout the society, insubordinate and critical elements ceased to exist, even in the form of dependent insubordination.

From this point on, the anxiety was projected externally in an explosive and violent manner, taking the form of atrocities abroad, such as the Nanking massacre. The logic of *amae* has an inherent tendency to divide the world clearly into two groups, an in-group in which it is met with a generous forbearance, and an out-group in which it is not. In a sense, it is rather similar to Max Weber's binary theory with its differentation between *Binnenmoral* and *Aussenmoral*.[19] In addition, the transfer of authority easily became what Professor Maruyama has termed the "transfer of oppression."[20] It was thus that oppressive measures were employed in a ferocious manner towards other nations. What ought to be borne in mind here is that German Nazism institutionalized hatred and massacre as a means to an end. In the Japanese case, the psychological impulse was an important factor in driving the Japanese to commit atrocities upon other nations. Whereas Nazism institutionalized "anxiety" itself by means of terror, propaganda, and by coercing everyone to be an accomplice in a crime and organizing hatred toward a specific scapegoat.[21] In Japan, the ruling system in the era of fascism was a result of institutionalizing *amae* by transforming anxiety into a sense of dependence.

Anxiety then was clearly the common factor in both the German and the Japanese cases. The difference was that the Japanese leaders sought, both directly and indirectly, to transform this into a sense of dependence. In other words, they tried to eliminate the anxiety by institutionalizing dependence, not by creating a solution to the anxiety itself. As can be seen in the child's self-awareness process, solution (conquest) of anxiety only becomes a matter of reality when a new possibility for overcoming that anxiety is opened up. We are told that such a possibility for gaining freedom involves "responsibility to be one's self as well as responsibility to others."[22] However, in a case where elimination of the anxiety is sought in sensual identification with the higher other, (e.g., with the national polity or with the emperor) and where a sense of dependency is deliberately institutionalized, *amae* produces a regression rather than a progression in responsibility. In this way, the system of irresponsibility which prevailed in Japan during the era of fascism was made all the more serious due to the particular way in which successful attempts were made to eliminate anxiety at home (the in-group venue) by transferring it abroad (the out-group venue).

Conclusion

As Emil Lederer observed, "Modern dictatorships like to compare themselves with, or call themselves, revolutions. But it would be difficult to explain the idea or the social structure which fascism meant to realize when it first developed. Furthermore, the masses on which they ride to power are institutionalized, and the consequences of this difference are decisive".[23] In fact modern dictatorships have had to cope with situations peculiar to mass society and to base themselves on mass mobilization. In this way "revolutionary" or "renovationist" slogans have been indispensable to dictatorships. Once the masses were tamed and institutionalized, they were, however, no longer permitted radical action of any kind whatsoever.

Certainly the above was true of both Germany and Japan but the way in which the masses were actually mobilized differed considerably in both countries. In Germany, a large scale dissolution of the old order was taking place and revolutionary groups had a considerable influence over the populace. Nazism, with its monolithic system of strong leadership, found it necessary to smash these pre-existing mass organizations and establish one of its own under the banner of "national revolution." In Japan, in contrast, the old social order was being dissolved only partially in terms of ideology and social structure and there were not so many influential leaders or revolutionary groups to be eliminated. The latter had been effectively dealt with at an early stage of the era of fascism. In this kind of situation, mobilization of the masses was carried out by absorbing even the leftists, who had been foiled in *their* attempts to bring about a revolution. Under the slogan of "renovation," these and other groups were the raw material of which the national organization was composed.

In Japan, radical renovationists outside the government can be perceived as somewhat analogous to the loud-voiced hawker at a circus show called the New Order Movement. The fact that such "hawkers" were needed indicated a momentum for historical change, a form of discontinuity. On the other hand, the shows performed inside the tent were produced by the elite of the old Japanese empire even though some new elements, the "renovation bureaucrats," were now included. These new elements, highly skilled in the techniques of management and control were better equipped to stage manage the acts so as to fit the public taste.

Ideologically speaking, the "renovationists" were incapable of severing connections with the past as in "revolution" and therefore were easily incorporated into the "imperial way" which was "empty" regarding political goals. The masses, their anxiety absorbed by the endless chain of authority, were domesticated by an endless chain of leadership. The radicals, seeking to substitute "renovation" for "revolution" came eventually to realize that they would not be permitted activities of their own even if such activities were in accord with the "renovation."

Such observations lead inevitably to the conclusion that tradition was more continuous in Japan than in Germany. This was true not only in regard to intensity but, more importantly, in the mode of its manifestation. It ought to be borne in mind that this strong continuity of tradition in the era of fascism seems to have some relevance to the continuity between this era and postwar Japanese society. In Germany, the Germans themselves undertook the task of de-Nazification. In Japan, the leaders of the era of fascism were purged, albeit temporarily, by the Occupation forces, not by the Japanese themselves. The bureaucracy, a major element of the "controlled state" was less affected by the purge than any of the other prewar elites, due to the decision by the Occupation authorities to rule through the existing machinery rather than establish an American military government. The depurging of the Japanese began during the Occupation and once the Occupation ceased, the prewar leaders were restored to their leading positions in society.

In addition to such overt aspects of continuity, many aspects continue beneath the surface. One example is that elements of various groups established by the Imperial Rule Assistance Association continue to exist. Enterprise unions contain elements of the Serve the State through Industry movement with the enterprise replacing the state as the focus of devotion. Agricultural cooperatives, so active in the postwar period, also contain a considerable residue of prewar elements. Space does not permit an extended discussion of this very important theme, but these groups, at least in their structure and leadership, are clearly not unconnected with the problems of prewar Japan. The problems faced by Japan, in the era of fascism, must not be taken lightly nor dismissed as the problems of a previous generation. These problems are still with us today and solutions must be found.

Notes

*This is a revised version of a paper presented in Japanese at the Japan Political Science Association's annual conference held at the Kanazawa University, Ishikawa Prefecture, in October 1975. It was presented with Prof. Karl Bracher's paper on "Tradition and Revolution in German National Socialism." I would like to express my gratitude to Professors Yasushi Yamaguchi and Hiroshi Kawahara for valuable comments and suggestions I received from them at the conference.

1. In this article, I use the term "era of fascism" in Japan to refer to the period from the latter half of the 1920s through to the end of World War II, with its peak in the 1930s. However, I shall not discuss here whether or not the political system of Japan in this period can be technically regarded as that of "fascism," since this is a question which directly touches on one's definition of "fascism" and I fear that once I start meddling with such a complex question I shall be unable to give sufficient consideration to the problem at hand.

2. I wonder whether the elements of discontinuity that existed in this period can be regarded as constituting a "revolution." This question also directly touches on the definition of "revolution." In the case of Germany, what Konard Heiden called a *Staatsstreich in Raten (Coup d'etat* in install-ments) may be regarded as a revolution because of the scope and depth of the changes it brought about. But the situation in Japan was far from even such a *Staatsstreich in Raten*. If we regard the transfer of power as one factor essential for a revolution, then the term "revolution" is not ade-quate for use in describing the situation that existed in Japan during the era of fascism. If we define a revolution more broadly to mean any social change which is wide in scope and deep in impact, then we may indeed use this word. But in that case, the term "social reform" sounds more adequate, given the fact that this is not the way the word for "revolution", *kakumei,* is usually understood in Japan.

In this connection, we should not overlook that in Germany Nazism used the slogan "national revolution," and the word "revolution" won public acceptance. This was not the case with Japan, though. While it is true that the rightists, too, advocated a revolution—as can be seen in the fact that a rightist organization Yūzon-sha issued its program in 1919 under the title *Kakumei Nihon no Kensetsu (Construction of a Revolutionary Japan),* the word *Kakumei* was quite unpopular and in the 1930s it became taboo. In view of this, I prefer the word *kakushin* ("renovation") which was used widely at that time to connote discontinuity. The very fact that the word *kakushin* was accepted unquestionably and used (but in a very vague sense) at that time is in itself an interesting topic for study. I will make further comments on this point later in the article.

Another, less crucial, reason why I choose not to use the word "revolu-tion" is that there are some attempts being made recently to discover an "indigenous theory of revolution" in the writings and actions of rightists in the era of fascism such as Ikki Kita. I will also touch on this point later.

3. S. N. Eisenstadt, *Tradition, Change and Modernity,* New York, John Wiley & Sons, 1973, pp. 47–72.
4. R. Dahrendorf, *Gesellschaft und Demokratie in Deutschland,* München, Piper, 1965, translated as *Society and Democracy in Germany,* London, Weidenfeld, 1967.
5. Showa Dōjinkai (ed.), *Showa Kenkyukai,* Keizai Ōraisha, 1968, pp. 304–305.
6. Yoshihiko Taniguchi, *Shintaisei no Riron,* Chikura Shobō, 1940, pp. 49–50.
7. Kishio Satomi, *Kokutai Ninshikiron,* Kokutai Kagakusha, 1929, pp. 134–136.
8. Kenji Maki, *Zotei Nihon Kokutai no Riron,* Yuhikaku, 1944, pp. 132–133.
9. Taniguchi, *op. cit.,* pp. 19f.
10. Kishio Satomi, *Tennō to Puroretaria,* Arususha, 1929, pp. 238, 231, 239.
11. Masami Sugihara, *Kokuminsoshiki no Seijiryoku,* Modan Nihonsha, 1940, p. 361.
12. Sugihara, *op. cit.,* pp. 372–373.
13. Shigeki Sano, *Saikin no Uyoku Undō ni tsuite* (On Recent Rightist Movements), 1938, included in *Gendaishi Shiryō* (Materials of Modern History), Vol. 23, Misuzu Shobō, 1974, p. 183.
14. Kurt Signer, a German national who taught in Japan from 1931 until 1939 when he was deported because of his Jewish lineage, makes a similar

remark: "Tennō (the emperor), who is himself nothing but a Medium, mediating between his ancestor gods on high and his subjects, not a figure in his own right." See Kurt Singer, *Mirror, Sword and Jewel,* edited with an introduction by Richard Storry, London, Crown-Hall, 1973, p. 109.

15. For the traditionally harmonious nature of Japanese society, see Takeshi Ishida, *Nihon no Seiji Bunka—Dōchō to Kyōso* (Japanese Political Culture—Conformity and Competition), Univ. of Tokyo Press, 1970, or see chapter two of this book.

16. Takeshi Ishida, "Urbanization and Its Impact on Japanese Politics—A Case of a Late and Rapidly Developed Country," *Annals of the Institute of Social Science,* no. 8, 1967, p. 1. For more details on urbanization in Japan, see this article.

17. Erich Fromm, *Escape from Freedom,* London, Routledge & Kegan Paul, 1942, p. 159.

18. Takeo Doi, *"Amae—A Key Concept for Understanding Japanese Personality Structure,"* R. J. Smith and R. K. Beardsley (eds.), *Japanese Culture: Its Development and Characteristics,* Chicago, Aldine Publishing Co., 1962; *idem., "Giri-Ninjō: An Interpretation"* R. P. Dore (ed.), *Aspects of Social Change in Modern Japan,* Princeton University Press, 1967.

19. Max Weber, *Wirtschaftsgeschichte,* Z. Veränderte Auflage, München, Leipzig, Duncker & Humblot, 1924, S.304.

20. Masao Maruyama, *Thought and Behavior in Modern Japanese Politics* (an expanded edition) edited by Ivan Morris, N.Y., Oxford University Press, 1969, p. 18.

21. Franz Neumann, *The Democratic and the Authoritarian State: Essays in Political and Legal Theory,* edited and with a preface by Herbert Marcuse, Glencoe, Ill., The Free Press, 1957, pp. 293–94.

22. Rollo May, *The Meaning of Anxiety,* N.Y., The Ronald Press, 1950, p. 234.

23. Emil Lederer, *State of the Masses, the Threat of the Classless Society,* N.Y., Howard Fertig, 1967, p. 226.

Part III

ESSAYS IN PEACE RESEARCH

CHAPTER SIX

Beyond the Traditional Concepts of Peace in Different Cultures

I

Countries at war always maintain that they are fighting "for peace." If the true meaning of peace were clear, perhaps many past wars could have been avoided. It is possible to argue that a lack of conceptual clarity may even be advantageous in the sense that it makes possible the inclusion of important human desires such as justice and prosperity. On the other hand, there is the danger that the concept can be used to justify any kind of war. In an age of nuclear weapons, we can no longer afford such justifications as "a war for peace" or a "just war" being used for starting one. Nuclear war is totally incapable of bringing about peace; it can only result in the destruction of mankind. Attention must be focused on two vital questions: How is it possible to prevent war, nuclear war or the highly technologically developed conventional war that is possible today, and how is it possible to achieve social justice without war?

What will be attempted here is an examination of the concept of "peace" and this may lead to a solution of the problem. We will also examine how past "wars for peace" have been successfully "justified." It might well be possible to eliminate the ambiguity in the concept of "peace" and thus prevent the abuse to which the concept is subjected, by providing an acceptable scientific definition. Such a method may well help to avoid the confusion which is always present in discussions of peace. This chapter will focus on the semantics of peace, how the word has been understood. Such a study may be a first step in the construction of a theoretical framework.

One major difficulty is that the concept of peace varies according to the culture. It is essential that the different concepts be clarified, and their common elements discovered.

Consider Japan in World War II. The nation's leaders stated that Japan was fighting for "peace in the East." At this time, those who refused to accept the Emperor system or who opposed the war, as well as communists, were labelled as *aka* (red) and vigorously suppressed. The clash between the concept of peace held by the leaders and the ideal of peace held by antiwar protestors can only be explained by reference to the traditional Japanese concept of peace. The "peace of the village" which is still a strong force in Japanese society, may help to clarify the characteristics of the traditional concept. In the national election of 1958, irregularities in an election campaign occurred in a certain village. A young girl, a native of the village, wrote to a newspaper exposing these irregularities, and the police began an investigation of the political machine operating in that area. As might be expected, the other villagers thought that this family had disturbed the "peace of the village."[1] The girl and her family were ostracized by the rest of the community; life became so unpleasant that the family had no choice other than to move away. Such occurrences were far more common before the war, but despite changes in society, it is important to note the continuity here. The "concept of peace" illustrated here clearly implies a preservation of the traditional system, customs and values, no matter how irrational are the foundations upon which they rest.

If analyses similar to the above were carried out it would greatly aid comparisons of the conceptual structure of peace in different cultures. One can understand from this why the Japanese pacifists were so fiercely attacked. Like the communists and the socialists, they appeared to disturb the social harmony and the conformity judged necessary for the war effort. As a result, it was possible to take the view that the pacifists were not "peaceful."

The cruelty of the Japanese in battle and the bravery exhibited in suicide tactics are well known. Such deeds were performed in order to achieve "peace in the East" despite the fact that the Japanese loved harmony and loathed conflict within their own society. Such inconsistencies can be explained by utilizing Max Weber's *Binnenmoral* (morality within the group) and *Aussenmoral* (morality beyond the group). The more intense the desire to maintain harmony among members of a society with a strong in-group tendency, the greater the impulse to battle any enemy which threatens the inner harmony from the outside. When such groups fight, they employ a morality toward the outside quite different from the morality employed toward the in-group. In a cultural context, when a whole country adopts a warlike attitude toward the outside, pacifists *must* resist. Japanese pacifists at this time were faced with two enemies, one based on the traditional idea of internal harmony and one based on the idea of "peace in the East." In such a situation it is perhaps understandable why Japan could not develop a system of "conscientious objection" in the prewar period. Only after defeat was such a thing possible, but, of course, it was incorporated indirectly in article 9 of the new Constitution as a renunciation of war.

Yet another example which may aid understanding of cultural conceptual differences regarding peace may be found in the approaches of Gandhi and Martin Luther King, Jr. In principle, their nonviolent direct action did not differ greatly. Gandhi deeply influenced King and they were both greatly influenced by Christianity and by Thoreau. They did have a difference in emphasis though and this seems to derive directly from the different cultural environment in which these men lived and worked. In order to make nonviolent direct action an effective political tool, they were forced to resolve certain quite different problems. Gandhi had to teach nonviolent *direct* action, whereas King had to teach *nonviolent* direct action. The differences undoubtedly stemmed from the different concepts of peace emerged from different traditions. India has its spiritual tradition of *ahiṁsā*, the killing of no living creature, and *śānti*, a well-ordered state of mind and usually translated as "peace" in English. As Romain Rolland stated in his biography of Gandhi, teaching nonviolent direct action to the Indian was significant in that it taught them to say No. In the United States on the other hand, Martin Luther King himself summed it up beautifully, "The eye-for-an-eye philosophy, the impulse to defend oneself from attack has always been held as the highest measure of American manhood. We are a nation that worships the frontier tradition, and our heroes are those who champion justice through violent retaliation against injustice."[2] This frontier tradition had part of its origins in the Judeo-Christian spiritual tradition, although it is undeniable that the teaching of Christ clearly upholds the principle of nonviolence.

Thus it seems natural that the Indian and the Judeo-Christian traditions should differ as to where they place the emphasis when teaching nonviolent direct action. Each has its own concept of peace. The Indian tradition has produced an inclination to preserve a tranquil state of mind, even accepting injustice, if necessary. The Judeo-Christian tradition, on the other hand, inclines toward fighting injustice and using force if necessary.

The Japanese tradition stands much nearer to the Indian than to the Judeo-Christian, partly because of the influence of Buddhism, which was introduced in Japan some twelve hundred years ago.

What follows is essentially a summary of *Politics for Peace* which I published in 1968. The approach adopted there was to ask: What must the Japanese do to maintain true peace? What merits does the Japanese moral tradition have which can serve as the foundation for this peace? What are the elements in Japanese tradition which may prove to be obstacles to such an effort? In order to do this, a cross-cultural comparison of the concepts of peace was undertaken. Originally intended for a Japanese audience, it is hoped that the findings may also prove to be of some use to people of other cultural backgrounds.

In addition, the study of the semantics of peace has a more general purpose. Differences in concepts of peace in different cultures indicate the inherent contradictions which exist. A way must be found not only to avoid "wars for peace" but to eliminate that passive quietism which maintains order and a calmness of mind, yet permits injustice to flourish. All cultures need to solve these particular problems and a semantic approach may prove profitable in efforts to reconcile the inherent contradictions in various concepts of peace.

Emphasis / Culture	The will of God, justice	Prosperity	Order	Tranquility of mind
Ancient Judaism	shālōm			
Greece		eirene		
Rome			Pax	
China (Japan)			ho p'ing or p'ing ho (heiwa)	
India				śānti

Our Diagram illustrates the original meanings of the concept of peace for the world's main cultures and also points out the differing emphases among them. The approach is open to criticism in that there has perhaps been too much of an oversimplification in their respective meanings. Also, their historical development has been rather neglected and probably too great an emphasis has been placed on differences rather than on similarities. The diagram itself ought to have been composed of overlapping circles rather than mutually exclusive boxes. For example, the table should not be taken to indicate, in the case of *shālōm*, that this does not imply tranquility of mind. The intention is simply to illustrate differences of emphasis. If the emphasis moves to the left, there will be an increase in the tendency to "fight for peace" and the possibility of taking positive action to realize justice will increase, stimulating again an increase in the dangerous tendency to "fight for peace." This dangerous tendency decreases as we move to the right of the table only to be replaced by another dangerous tendency, passive quietism, which may permit injustice and tacitly approve situations that may result in war. What follows is a brief explanation of the concepts of peace and a clarification of the relationships among them. All the concepts treated here are denoted by terms usually translated as "peace" in English. There are, however, other terms related to nonviolence, such as *ashiṁsā*. In fact, why *ahiṁsā*, rather than *śānti*, is not translated as "peace" is an interesting question. One answer may well be that terms translated as peace usually denote vital goals in life. *Ahiṁsā* or other terms indicating nonviolence have usually been considered as means rather than ends in themselves. A consideration of the relationships between these two groups is certainly necessary, but they cannot be included in the same chart due to the difference in dimension. This chapter will therefore only consider those terms usually translated as "peace."

II

Shālōm

G. Kittel says that *shālōm* and *eirene* differ in their original forms: the former denotes a quality of relationship *(Verhältnis)* and the latter a state of being *(Zustand)*.[3] *Shālōm* stresses the unity in *berîth* (convenant) and the realization of Jehovah's divine will, and it brings about justice and prosperity. J. Pederson explains that *shālōm* and *berîth* are inseparable, and they were sometimes used interchangeably.[4] *Berîth* is superior to family or blood relationships, although they precede it. The creation of unity in the convenant was the indispensable condition for realizing *shālōm* and was even thought to be *shālōm* itself.

Shālōm was not a state of being—on the contrary, it was a condition which the people created through their own initiative. For example, the realization of *shālōm* among the people signified the conclusion of a contract among them; more specifically, it was the contract by which males became circumcised members of the Jewish faith. (This is why *berîth* also means circumcision.) Max Weber says that Jehovah was the God of contractual union *(Bundenskriegsgott):* Israel was based on this contract with, and was supported and headed by, Jehovah.[5] If *shalōm* is a contract with Jehovah, it follows that it denotes a living and dynamic relationship and not a static condition.

We have good reason to believe that *shalōm* was regarded as referring not mainly to a state of mind but rather to politicoeconomic relations. The Israelites, as a nomadic people of the desert, were exposed to the danger of attack from outside and were threatened by the possibility of dissolution from within. Under the internal contract they had to present a strong united front against the outside. *Shalōm* implied that which was gained in battle and not given by nature; specifically, it was given in battle by God. It was the process which revealed the divine will through the contract with God. In this respect *shalōm* was not a state where all tensions were finally relieved.

Thus *shalōm* did not necessarily oppose the concept of war, since it sometimes signified victory in battle.

The Arab countries which suffered great losses in the Six Day War with Israel (1967) share the same historical origin as their bitter foe, Judaism, and have much in common. The name of Islam, *al-Islàm* in Arabic, means "to be at peace" as well as "to give absolute devotion." Just as in ancient Judaism, it also signified fighting for the revelation of God's will.

The Moslems interpret "a holy war" *(jihād)* as "a fight for the code of Allah." And yet the so-called bellicosity of Islam—indicated in the slogan, "The Koran in the left hand, a sword in the right hand" is from the Moslem point of view a biased Christian interpretation. Muhammad Ali, who translated the Koran into English, asserts that Islam is truly a "religion of peace."

The fierce antagonism between Israel and the Arab countries has been attended by hatred on a national scale ever since the formation of Israel as a state. This seems to have been caused partly by a common tradition of monotheism and a similar militant concept of peace as a realization of justice by the divine will.

We must consider the Graeco-Roman influence on Christianity, but that it has also inherited the shalomic concept of peace (realization of justice and achievement of divine will) is shown in the idea of the *bellum justum* (just war) and the Crusades.

Eirene

Eirene, which is thought to have its origin in a word meaning union, denoted a state, while *shalōm* denoted a relationship. It stressed the importance of unity and order. It was thought to produce prosperity, although it did not directly signify prosperity. In this sense, *shālōm* and *eirene* have something in common. Above all we must not forget that the relation between order and peace gained importance with the development of the *polis*. There was already a marked contrast between the peace among Hellenes and war against the non-Hellenes (i.e., the "barbarians") long before the time of Persian Wars (fifth century B.C.).[6] Plato's day and age was no exception to this way of thinking. Plato said that disorder in Hellas was worse than a war against outsiders, since barbarians were the natural enemy of the Hellenes.

Isocrates took up this concept of peace which stressed inner order, and maintained that peace should be understood in close relationship to democracy, thus criticizing those political parties that advocated war. Democracy in the Greek *polis* did not include slaves and women and thus differed greatly from our present system. Still, Isocrates warned that what democracy they had would be destroyed by war. His treatise was the first to discuss the relationship between peace and democracy from the viewpoint that there can be no democratic order and prosperity without peace.[7]

Pax

The Roman concept of *pax* is similar to the Greek concept of *eirene*, in that it denotes a state. As in *Pax Romana*, it was often regarded as a state of good order and absence of war, although it sometimes included a state of good order achieved by conquest. It also signified a legal relation based on a pact (the English word "pact" itself is from *pax*). However, the Roman pact was a secular one based on Roman law, unlike the concept of the covenant, *berîth*. Another difference between *pax* and *shālōm* is the association of the former with a tranquil state of mind: there is the expression *pax animi*, peace of mind.

Sānti

Compared with the concepts of peace discussed above, traditional concepts of peace in India and China are rather different.

In India there is *śānti*, usually translated "peace," which means a well-ordered state of mind; and there is also *ahiṁsā*, which means rejection of killing, nonviolence. The principle of *ahiṁsā*, taking no life, animal or human, was employed by Mahatma Gandhi as a social and political weapon for social reform and independence.

Unlike the concepts of peace considered so far, traditional *śānti* had nothing to do with political conditions. The Indians had other political concepts: and *vigraha* was war as national policy, or hostility leading to war; *samdhi* was a state of no *vigraha*. They also had a concept *śama,* meaning a well-governed social order.[8] A tranquil state of mind was indeed a part of the Roman concept of peace, but it was considered mainly within the political context: good order within, and absence of war without. The concept of *śānti* was regarded only as tranquillity of mind, completely separated from all political relations.

In fact, although Hinduism, Buddhism, and Jainism earnestly preached *śānti,* the political struggles in the course of which the Gautama clan was ruined, lasted for thousands of years. Max Weber says that this characteristic is a special feature of Indian religious ethics, aimed at escape from this world.

Under the caste system rigidly maintained in that society, not to die in bed (but on the battlefield) was the highest desire of the warrior caste *Kṣatriya* to which the political rulers belonged. The *Dharmaśāstra* said that the warrior was allowed to resort to arms only when all other means failed and that his conduct in battle should be limited by *dharma* (law, duty). However, the *Arthaśāstra,* which deals with the education of the monarch, explains how to weaken the enemy and achieve victory. The highest caste, *Brāhmana,* was interested only in spiritual matters, not in the secular world.

The reign of King Aśoka (reigned approximately 268–232 B.C.), who followed the principles of Buddhism and whose government was based on Buddhist ideals, was quite exceptional in the long history of India.

Ho P'ing

Chinese ethics, represented by Confucianism, assumed an affirmative attitude to the secular world, unlike traditional Indian ethics, the aim of which was to escape from the world. They seem to be located at opposite poles in this respect. However, concepts of peace in China and India have placed similar emphasis on state of mind. We know from many examples in the Chinese classics that the term *ho p'ing* (peace) corresponded to a well-ordered state of mind.

Political order, which India was unable to achieve, was usually called *ho p'ing;* but the term *p'ing ho,* which denoted a state of mind, was also sometimes used to indicate a state of political order. Consequently *ho p'ing* and *p'ing ho,* which are written with the same characters in reverse order, seem to have similar original meaning, even though the frequency of their usage varies with time and place. In this connection, it must not be forgotten that natural and social phenomena were considered to be continuous. Identification between cosmic order and social order has been clearly pointed out by Max Weber as a characteristic of the Confucian outlook.[9] Social phenomena were often identified with natural phenomena. For example, the crops were believed to depend on rites performed by the ruler, and natural disasters such as floods were thought to spring from failure of the ruler to maintain harmony with nature. Max Weber says that this characteristic is common to both China and India. *Ho p'ing* was regarded as obedience to the whole cosmic order, from which social and natural order were inseparable.

Heiwa

The concept of *heiwa* (peace) in Japan has been influenced by China and India as have other aspects of her culture. *Heiwa* bears a closer relation to *p'ing ho* than to the Indian concept. It is written with the same Chinese characters as *p'ing ho* despite the different pronunciation. Besides, both *heiwa* and *p'ing ho* are related to political order. Since Japan had no caste system and had been influenced by Buddhism for many centries, this influence had extended both to the *samurai* (warriors) and to the farmers. For one thing, as the *samurai* were deeply affected by Zen Buddhism, some of the more courageous ones grew dubious of the practice of killing and finally became Buddhist monks, giving up their swords. Moreover, to those who did not give up the calling of *samurai,* the meaning of fighting lay not in killing others but in dying bravely, to which end they disciplined their minds.

Heiwa is apt to be understood as an adaptation to the social order as in Confucian ethics, because it is closely related to harmony, but it also implies a tranquil state of mind. Furthermore, it places an emphasis on emotion, which distinguishes Japanese Confucianism from classical Chinese Confucianism. Another characteristic is the aesthetic factor added to harmony in which social order and individual emotional feeling are respectively involved. This probably derives from the tradition of Shinto, where aesthetic factors, for example "purity," were dominant.

The above outlines, taken from ancient Judean culture, Greco-Roman culture, and from India, China and Japan, may perhaps be interpreted as showing a considerable lack of caution on the part of the author. Indeed, some might consider it impertinent to discuss so many different cultural concepts without a deep understanding of all those cultures. However, the intention was not to provide detailed descriptions of the concepts of peace in each culture. This study had the rather more limited objective of attempting to clarify their differences of emphasis. This was attempted in the belief that such a venture would have some significance when one considers the problems surrounding the concept of peace, and peace itself, at this time.

The positive orientation toward justice in *shalōm*, the stress on good order in *eirene* and *pax* and the emphasis on state of mind in *śānti*, *p'ing ho*, and *heiwa* are all significant components of peace and, to some extent, each implies the other. The differences of emphasis have been somewhat exaggerated for the sake of comparison. However, certain difficulties do exist. The three factors—realization of justice, maintenance of good order, and tranquility of mind—are, in fact, likely to conflict with each other: Injustice must be opposed in order to realize justice. This in turn may threaten good order and tranquility of mind. Too great an emphasis on peace of mind and harmony may lead not only to a rejection of violence but also to the rejection of any criticism of the established order. This results in a peace-at-any-price attitude which tolerates injustice.

When Gandhi came into contact with the Christian concept of peace, he selected many of its good points and added them to the Indian concept, which with its emphasis on tranquility, was a concept which nurtured political apathy. He set out to eliminate many of the shortcomings in the Indian concept and further developed the traditional concept of *ahiṁsā*. In this way he eventually created the principle of nonviolent direct action.

Martin Luther King, facing similar problems in a different, a Judeo-Christian culture, managed to find a tool for overcoming the frontier principle of fighting for justice with guns. He found his answer in Gandhian principles and became a leading advocate of nonviolent direct action.

III

Thus far, an attempt has been made to explain the characteristics of the concept of peace in different cultures and to point out some of the inherent difficulties which exist when one considers peace. In the original Japanese version of this essay what followed was a historical example, moving from the Christian attitude toward the *bellum justum* to a consideration of the historical development of methods of controlling war, including a discussion of Saint Pierre, Rousseau, and Kant. The Quaker and Marxist views of war were also considered. But, since such matters are quite familiar to Western readers they have been omitted here. Instead, what follows are the author's views, as a Japanese, on nonviolent direct action.

The contradictions inherent in the concept of peace can only be overcome by seeking peace through nonviolent action. But the question remains as to whether resort to nonviolent action can really achieve justice. It is a problem which has plagued mankind since the dawn of history. In today's world, a solution is more urgent than ever.

It is naturally easier to prove the *necessity* of nonviolent direct action in the present situation than it is to prove the *feasibility* of such an approach. Even in such countries as the United States where parliamentary democracy is highly developed, social injustices have proved difficult to eradicate. A turbulent protest movement was necessary to force the system to tackle the problem of improving the situation of the black American. As a result, legislation was passed guaranteeing this ethnic group the right to vote, among other rights, but much more pressure is needed to abolish the various forms of segregation and inequalities which continue to exist. There are many Black Americans and members of other ethnic groups who feel impatient with the delays and some of these have advocated—and practiced—violent protest. But violent protest results in an escalation of violence between the protesters and the government. In terms of political effect, violence cannot succeed in the long run. In Japan recently, violent protests by students were used as a pretext for an increase in police armaments and in the end the student protests were harshly suppressed. It should be apparent to all that we no longer live in the age of the French Revolution or the Paris Commune, when street fighting was still effective.

Although violent protest is inappropriate, both morally and pragmatically, this does not mean that *protest* is unnecessary or ineffective. On the contrary, protest is necessary in order to prevent democracy from stagnation. The principal danger involved in the *violent* form of protest is that it may lead to the breakdown of democratic government and to the creation of something much worse. The only effective means of achieving social justice and at the same time maintaining democratic procedures may well lie in protest but in protest by nonviolent direct action.

This strategy must be applied also to the international system since the potential escalation of violence in this area may easily reach a point where neither side can survive. But at the same time, injustice in the international arena must not be tolerated. The major difficulty here is that these sovereign states possess—or in a sense are possessed by—

huge military establishments. There would seem to be no reason why a man should be labeled a murderer and punished for taking another's life within the borders of his country, while one who commits the same act outside that country's borders during war is rewarded as a patriot. Martin Luther King was absolutely correct when he pointed out that one ought to consistently apply the "philosophy of nonviolence from the streets of Selma and Memphis to the rice paddies of the Mekong Delta and the jungles of Vietnam."[10]

However, nonviolent direct action *within* a nation and *between* nations involves a common difficulty: There is no historical evidence that justice has ever been achieved by such methods. In the former case, a careful investigation of the philosophy and strategy of Mahatma Gandhi and Martin Luther King provides some useful hints and guidelines. The work of Joan Bondurant in this field, *Conquest of Violence* (1965), is particularly important. Here however the discussion will be limited to examining Japan as a possible model for an unarmed, neutral country.

Japan was probably the first country in history ever to include in its Constitution a clause which renounces war.[11] How can Japan succeed in providing the first example of an unarmed—yet not "vulnerable"—nation? One must first consider the present political situation in Japan. The Japanese in addition to having a "peace Constitution" also exhibit a deep and widespread opposition to war. In a poll conducted by the Japan Broadcasting Company (NHK) in 1968 in answer to the question "What are you most concerned about?" the war in Vietnam was ranked second at 51 percent behind high prices at 78 percent. (In this poll, respondents could submit more than one issue.) This does not necessarily mean that the Japanese are particularly interested in peace as a principle. It means rather that the problem of war and peace is in no way remote from their daily lives. In the first place, they are extremely sensitive about war because of their experience of both conventional and atomic bombing. In 1967 the number of A-bomb survivors was 313,161 and this was only the official government total. Also, the war in Vietnam meant an increase in the problems caused by the presence of American military bases, airplane crashes, misconduct by G.I.'s, and prostitution. But despite such attitudes among the people, the Japanese government remained committed to the Vietnam War in that she provided the United States with military bases under an obligation deriving from the security treaty between the two countries. Japan has had its Self-Defense Forces, created by the Occupation authorities in 1950 at the time of the Korean War. With the passage of time, this "illegitimate" armed force, has received more and more acceptance by the populace. At the end of 1968, 17 percent of the respondents in an *Asahi* newspaper public opinion poll thought that the SDF was unconstitutional while 40 percent considered that it did not contravene the Constitution.[12]

The acceptance of the Self-Defense Forces does not in itself imply approval of a full-fledged army, navy and air force. This is because many of the respondents perceived the Self-Defense Forces to be something other than a military force. For instance, the *Yomiuri* newspaper at the end of 1968 obtained the following results in an opinion poll. In answer to the question, "How should we deal with the present Self-Defense Forces?" 12.3 percent stated that they should be strengthened, 6 percent that they should be abolished, 43.6 percent that they should be retained in their present form and 26.3 percent that they should be transformed into a construction corps. The latter figure is most significant in that, even among those who believe the SDF should remain in its present form there are a considerable number who believe the main *raison d'être* of the forces is not military but chiefly rescue work in times of disasters. [13] In a 1966 government survey, 80 percent thought the SDF most useful for rescue work in disaster areas and other nonmilitary cooperation with civilian sectors. [14]

The ruling Liberal Democratic party, which has been in power throughout almost the entire postwar era, has always intended to revise the Constitution in order to provide the basis for a constitutional, full-fledged military force. So far they have been unsuccessful, due mainly to the strength of popular feeling in support of the peace Constitution. This is well expressed in such opposition party slogans as, "Boys, don't take up arms! Women, don't send your sons and sweethearts to the battlefield!" An *Asahi* opinion poll at the end of 1968 showed that only 19 percent favored the revision of the Constitution in order to permit full-fledged military forces, while 64 percent opposed such a move.

One area in which there is particular sensitivity is in the area of nuclear armaments. In the *Asahi* opinion poll, 67 percent felt that the American nuclear umbrella actually endangered Japan while only 12 percent thought it improved their safety. As to whether Japan would be more secure if it had its own nuclear weapons, 21.4 percent answered yes while 55.6 percent thought it decreased security. In that same poll, 49.7 percent thought that war was not permissible even in self defense. Such facts leave little doubt that the "peace Constitution" has taken deep root in Japan and is a major factor in the widespread antipathy to war of any sort. In a country such as Japan, where the majority are not in favor of a full-fledged military, the question naturally arises as to how Japan ought to be defended, how her security can be guaranteed. To answer this question, the *Tokyo Shimbun* newspaper poll in 1968 revealed that 30.4 percent felt that security ought to be guaranteed by the UN, 20.3 percent by a policy of unarmed neutrality, 16.7 percent by maintaining the US-Japan security treaty, and 15.1 percent by strengthening the Self-Defense Forces.[15]

Although 73.9 percent of those interviewed in the *Asahi* poll felt that Japan should maintain its security by its own efforts, only a minority felt that it should be done by strengthening the SDF. In fact, quite a large number felt that unarmed neutrality offered the best solution. However, in the popular mind it is not at all clear just how Japan's security can be guaranteed by a policy of unarmed neutrality. Before dealing with this particular problem, though, something must be said about the major obstacle in Japan's progress towards unarmed neutrality. It is the policy taken by the government which diverges sharply from the popular attitudes described above. Many people are disenchanted, even angry, with a governing party which continually chooses to ignore public opinion, which involved Japan in the Vietnam War, and which has continued to strengthen the SDF, but there is little likelihood of a change in the ruling party in the near future.

One important reason for the continued existence of what in effect is a semigovernment party is that at election time many voters are concerned less with the policies put forward by candidates than with the short range return they can expect from a particular candidate if elected. Naturally, candidates from a governing party are in a much better position when it comes to "pork barrel" politics; they are better able to influence the allocation of budget funds to a certain group or district. The majority of voters are enlightened enough to perceive which candidate can provide the better short term return but not sophisticated enough to realize that the long term results are far more important.[16]

This sort of practical attitude is sustained by the traditional attitude toward group harmony. Although, at the national level, the conformity centered on the Emperor was shattered by the defeat in war, group conformity still remains strong in diverse areas of society. "The interest of the district" or the "interest of the group" can easily provide the leverage to mold group conformity into a bloc vote. The ostracism of the girl and her family, mentioned earlier, is an example of such conformity. This sort of group conformity, originating in communal rural life (the peace of the village) was often reflected in the traditional political apathy which tended towards passive obedience to local bosses and other superiors. Although there has been a decline in both traditional communal ties and traditional political apathy, this has been replaced by an increase in the solidarity of groups devoted to more practical interests and also by a new type of political apathy arising from the nature of mass society.

These new tendencies are, in different ways, related to the traditional Japanese concept of peace, which is intertwined with that of harmony. Harmony within the group means that each member must behave as the others, thus emphasizing the importance of unanimity. In the case of political apathy, "peace" tends to mean that, in order to maintain a "peaceful" individual or family life, one must not "rock the boat." This sort of political apathy, arising out of the isolation and anxiety endemic to mass society is by no means peculiar to Japan. However, these modern concepts remain intertwined with the traditional concept of peace. Today we must end this traditional fusion—and confusion—of the concepts of peace and harmony. What is now necessary is the emergence of a nonconformity which can combat this weakness in the traditional Japanese concept of peace.

In present day Japan there is clearly a strong feeling of resentment against the established social order, from the parliamentary system to the bureaucratized hierarchy. This feeling has been expressed in the protest movements against the government or against any authority considered to be a part of the established order. Radical students have in the past organized violent protest movements against the U.S.-Japan security treaty, against American military bases, and even against the construction of new airports. They have also fought against the university administrations which they see as part of the establishment. No doubt their violence is a projection of serious discontent. It is probably also true that the creation of conflict is necessary in order to overcome traditional conformism. However, there are two major difficulties resulting from the violent actions of the students. One is caused by the violence itself. Acts of violence can never be effective since they can always be suppressed by a stronger physical force, the police. And in the unlikely event of the police being overcome, there is the danger of the country falling into anarchy—where democracy cannot survive. The other difficulty arises from the need to maintain solidarity within these nonconformist groups, which leads back to conformism again.

If the tradition of group conformity is really so strong, and can be found even within opposition groups such as labor unions, where can we find an emergent nonconformism? As the strength of alienation grows in mass society, a mistrust in the authority of group conformity has emerged as a result of the stagnation created by that very conformity. The people's dependence on the groups to which they belong is so strong that their disillusionment is a very serious matter. Peace organizations have become victims of this tendency. As they have grown in size, they have also become bureaucratized. Factional disputes among the parties on the left have also been a cause of fragmentation in peace movements. Increased political apathy is one result of this. Yet another result has been that some people, as yet small in number, discontented with the state of the existing peace organizations, have begun to realize that the improvement of present conditions can only lie in their own hands. They have come to realize that, regardless of the organization they belong to, they must take the initiative themselves. In certain cases, such is their distrust of the leadership of any large organization that they have begun forming very small groups controlled by the members of the groups themselves. This had been happening particularly in terms of peace and civic movements. In fact, for the first time in Japanese history, Japan has a multitude of voluntary groups, voluntary in the strict sense, to campaign for peace.

The numbers involved are, as yet, few compared with the large organizations. Two examples give us some idea as to how the smaller groups are on the increase. One is the working together of more than two hundred of these groups to protest the war in Vietnam; the result was a demonstration involving 10,000 marchers in Tokyo on June 15, 1968. The other example is the movement organized by a number of peace groups to distribute the English translation of a Japanese correspondent's reports from Vietnam. A series of ten articles by this correspondent had appeared in the *Asahi* in 1967 and 3,390 letters were received by the editor expressing readers' views. As a result of an appeal in one of the letters for the articles to be translated and sent abroad, particularly to the United States, a movement emerged which succeeded in dispatching 30,000 copies within one year.

While other examples could be cited,[17] it is still too early to be overly optimistic about the growth of civic concern in Japan. The trend towards overcoming the weakness in the traditional concept of "peace" is still limited to a small enlightened segment of society. Hopefully the people's wishes for peace will eventually force a reticent government to abide by the ideals of the Constitution which states: "Never again shall we be visited by the horrors of war through the action of government." Only then will Japan be strong. Naturally, the aim of this essay is to suggest that only through constant resistance to the government—by nonviolent means—can this be achieved. If nonviolent resistance can control their own government then the Japanese people need not be overly concerned with a lack of armaments. They could then extend their principles to encompass the international and domestic spheres, using the same method of nonviolent resistance.

Postscript

Since the above article was written in 1969, various changes have taken place. One of the most remarkable is that the students, who formed the core of earlier protest movements, have become quiet and conservative during the 1970s. (This is also true of many other industrialized societies.) The majority of the students in the University of Tokyo a decade ago supported opposition parties; today the majority support the conservative ruling party. Nationwide public opinion polls indicate that 70 to 80 percent of interviewees in various polls approve the existence of the Self-Defense Forces under the "peace Constitution," although it must be added that more than 40 percent of those approving of the forces still think that their *raison d'être* is rescue work during disasters. Despite the fact that the people who support the "peace Constitution" continue to form 60 to 70 percent of the interviewees in various public opinion polls, the Self-Defense Forces have been growing at such a rate that Japan's defense expenditure is ranked the eighth in the world. This fact clearly shows that the popular support for the "peace Constitution" alone is not sufficient to check the growth of military power.

The militarization under the "peace Constitution" has created a fear among Asian neighbors that Japan's economic dominance may become military dominance again. The right wing in Japan, particularly after the Russian invasion of Afghanistan, has become more vocal, demanding a stronger military. Some leading business figures are also pressing for an increased military budget. One of them even proposed to introduce a conscription system. The recent American pressure to increase Japan's military expenditure has accelerated the tendency toward strengthening the military.

The general populace is not necessarily in favor of such a tendency, but few serious protest movements are taking place. This is chiefly due to the conservative mood or apathy prevailing in our affluent society. Against this conservative background, even some intellectuals are advocating a stronger military force to defend the nation. They argue that unarmed neutrality is simply a dream in today's world. Those Japanese peace researchers who believe in pacifism are now facing a difficult task in dissuading these so-called realists.

Before dealing with the pacifist view of this problem, a brief mention is necessary concerning the development of peace research in Japan. Immediately after the first meeting of the International Peace Research Association in 1964, a group of Japanese scholars attempted to establish a study group responding to the world trend for peace research and to the need for peace research in Japan. The Japan Peace Research Group emerged and has been publishing *Peace Research in Japan* (in English) annually. This is merely a small group composed of less than fifty scholars, maintaining their independence from any political force or movement. In 1973 a larger organization called the Peace Studies Association of Japan, with a few hundred members, was formed and has been publishing books and journals.

As the numbers of peace researchers increases in Japan, their opinions have become diversified. Since it is difficult to summarize these opinions, it would be better to indicate the author's own view with the hope that it can, to a certain extent, be accepted as representative.

In contemporary war, it is impossible to make a distinction between civilians and the military. This can clearly be exemplified by the case of Okinawa which was the only place in Japan itself where fighting took place during World War II. More civilians, including women and children, were killed during the battle, than were men in uniform. In such a densely populated country as Japan, once a battle is fought civilians will suffer greatly. Therefore, a *nonviolent* civilian resistance, which would still require personal sacrifice, is much less destructive.

Of course, nonviolent resistance is the last line of defense once an invasion takes place. One could easily argue that in order to prevent an invasion, a certain measure of deterrence is necessary. That may be correct, but how can the maintainance of physical power for deterrence be achieved without causing an arms race? In relation to this, a proposal made by Professor Yoshikazu Sakamoto is suggestive. His idea is to put the present Self-Defense Forces under the command of an international agency to make it genuinely defensive and to help ensure peace—and relieve the fears of Japan's neighbors. As far as strenthening one's military power is concerned, it is very difficult to make it purely "defensive." But if controlled by an international agency, a military force can be "guaranteed" defensive and the danger of an arms race can be avoided.[18] The author believes that Professor Sakamoto's idea can be easily coordinated with his own views on domestic pacifism.

Of course, we are open to any other proposals as to how to deal with our situation. What is important is to find a creative idea that will free us from the fixed idea that a stronger military force will provide greater security.

Notes

1. The girl published a book: Satsuki Ishikawa, *Murahachibu no ki (A Story of Ostracism)*. Tokyo, Rironsha, 1953. A brief description of the affair can be found in *Time,* Aug. 25, 1952.
2. Martin Luther King Jr., *Why We Can't Wait,* New York, Harper & Row, 1963, pp. 27–28.
3. *Theologisches Wörterbuch zum Neuen Testament,* herausgegeben von Gerhart Kittel. vol. 2, Stuttgart, Kohlhammer, 1935, S.400f.
4. Johs, Pedersen, *Israel: Its Life and Culture,* 1–2, Oxford University Press, 1926, pp. 263f.
5. Max Weber, *Gesammelte Aufsätze zur Religionssoziologie,* vol. 2, Tübingen, Mohr, 1923, S.126f.
6. Wallace E. Caldwell, *Hellenic Concepts of Peace,* New York, Columbia University Press, 1919, p.69.
7. Isocrates, *On the Peace,* with an English translation by George Norlin, vol.2., London, The Loeb Classical Library, 1929.
8. J. Duncan & M. Derrett, "The Maintenance of Peace in the Hindu World: Practice and Theory," *The Indian Year Book of International Affairs,* vol. 8. 1959, pp. 361–387.
9. Max Weber, *Gesammelte Aufsätze zur Religionssoziologie* Vol. 1, Tübingen, Mohr, 1922, S.441.
10. *New York Times,* April 7, 1968.
11. Article Nine of the Constitution clearly states: "Aspiring sincerely to an international peace based on justice and order, the Japanese people forever renounce war as a sovereign right of the nation and the threat or use of force as a means of settling international disputes.

    In order to accomplish the aim of the preceding paragraph, land, sea, and air forces, as well as other war potential, will never be maintained. The right of belligerency of the state will not be recognized."
12. Published in the *Asahi Shimbun,* January 5, 1969. This poll used a random nationwide sample of 3,000 persons over 20 years of age.
13. The *Yomiuri Shimbun,* January 1, 1969. The sample of 10,000 interviewees was chosen by stratified random sampling from persons between 19 and 79 years of age.
14. Asahi shimbun anzenhoshō chōsaki (The Asahi shimbun Research Group on the Security Problem), *70-nen no seiji kadai (Political Tasks in 1970),* Asahi shimbunsha, 1967, p. 162.
15. The *Tokyo Shimbun,* January 1, 1969. This poll used a random nationwide sample of 3,000 persons over 20 year of age. For more detailed information about Japanese public opinion on foreign policy, see Takeshi Ishida, "Japanese Public Opinion and Foreign Policy," *Peace Research in Japan,* ed. by the Japan Peace Research Group, Tokyo, 1967.
16. For more detailed characteristics of Japanese society, see Takeshi Ishida, *Japanese Society,* New York, Random House, 1971.
17. For more detail, see Takeshi Ishida, "Emerging or Eclipsing Citizenship—

A Study of Change in Political Attitudes in Postwar Japan," *The Developing Economics,* vol. 6, no. 4 (Dec. 1968), Tokyo, Institute of Asian Economic Affairs.

18. For more detailed content of Sakamoto's proposal, see Yoshikazu Sakamoto, "Alternative Security Systems," to be published as one of the Working Papers of the World Order Models project.

CHAPTER SEVEN

Japan's Changing Image of Gandhi

I

In Japan, as in India, the image of Gandhi has varied, both over time and from individual to individual. It is perhaps only natural that the teaching of such a great man should be subject to a wide range of interpretations. The aim of this chapter is to identify some of the main elements in the Japanese interpretations of Gandhi and his works. It is hoped that the chapter will also shed light on Japanese views of India and of Asia as a whole.

The first Japanese language biography of Gandhi was by Taketane Takata, *Seiyu Gandhi* (1922).[1] *Sei* means sage and *yu* means hero—an attempt to translate the Hindu title *mahatma*. Despite the fact that *Seiyu* differed in some respects from *mahatma,* the term continued in use until the end of the last war. Thus, when the Japanese translation of Romain Rolland's biography of Gandhi was published in 1942, the title was *Seiyu Gandhi*.[2] In 1943, Yonejiro Noguchi published yet another biography using the same title.[3]

The title *seiyu* reflects the Japanese image of Gandhi as that of a traditional *fakir*. The term gave the impression of a virtuous man possessing tranquility of mind. Thus, the essence of Gandhi's teachings was often characterized as being the principle of "nonresistance," i.e., passivity. Curiously, even though many of Gandhi's Japanese biographers described in detail Gandhi's activities in resisting British rule, the term "nonresistance" continued to be used to describe the essence of Gandhian ideas.

One famous writer, Setsurei Miyake, in his introduction to Takata's biography, wrote: "Gandhi's idea is nothing new. It belongs to an old Indian tradition, and broadly speaking, it also has something in common with Chinese Taoism, Russian Tolstoyism and even with a part of the Christian tradition. It can be called the principle of nonresistance, if

137

such a definition does not produce misunderstanding."[4] Miyake did not elaborate on how Gandhian ideas could be compared to Taoism but it becomes clear if we take other Japanese images of Gandhi into account.

In prewar Japan, there existed the tendency to emphasize the element of anticivilization in Gandhian ideas. For example, Tadashi Shigemori wrote in 1922 that Gandhi proposed a return to nature.[5] Another biographer of Gandhi, Takanobu Murobuse, writing in 1933, stated that none of Gandhi's activities could be understood without an understanding of the fundamental point that they all derived from his total rejection of modern civilization.[6] He went on to explain that a new sun would arise and throw its benign light on the soil still free from the poisonous effects of modern civilization, itself in its death throes. Such an interpretation of Gandhi, combined with the idea of nonresistance produced in the minds of many Japanese an image rather close to that of the Chinese sage in that the latter believed in a kind of quietism or immobilism emphasising the importance of tranquility of mind. This image was certainly misleading if we pause to consider the strenuous nonviolent direct action employed by Gandhi. Nor is it correct to classify Gandhi as an advocate of the principle of anticivilization. As he himself explained, he did not reject machines as such but was against the misuse of machines if this resulted in the prosperity of the few at the expense of the many.

Among Japanese who laid emphasis on the spiritual side of Gandhi, some compared him with Tolstoy. In the period immediately after World War I, when Japanese intellectuals were deeply influenced by Western ideas, an idealistic tendency became fashionable. Riichiro Hoashi's *Religious Thoughts of Tolstoy and Gandhi* (1922), reflected such a trend.[7] In the book, the author found a similarity between Tolstoy and Gandhi in their opposition to the egoism prevailing in modern civilization. Tadashi Shigemori also pointed out that there was a similarity between the two men in their rejection of violence, private property and modern civilization. Shigemori went on to call Gandhi "an apostle of love and non-resistance."[8] Clearly, however, such interpretations missed the great difference dividing Tolstoy and Gandhi: "With Tolstoy nonviolence meant a quite different thing from Gandhian *satyagraha*. It meant avoidance of all force in any form. It was in no case a technique for mass positive constructive action."[9]

Some of those who emphasised the religious aspects of Gandhian ideas found there an element of opposition to Marxism, the latter being considered atheistic. Riichiro Hoashi and Kan Fukunaga are representative of such thinkers.[10]

All these views, perhaps influenced by the usage of the term "nonre-sistance," ignored the important role that political activism played in Gandhism. This usage continued into the early 1940s despite the fact that more accurate information concerning the nature and scope of the Gandhian movement in India began to filter into Japan. This new evidence eventually produced a distinction between passive resistance and *satygraha* and yet the old image persisted. Why nonresistance persisted in the minds of Japanese writers on Gandhi is extremely difficult to explain. One reasonable possibility is that such writers sought to explain Gandhian ideas by reference to the traditional conceptual framework of Japan, which, however, did not provide for the concept of nonviolent direct action. Even in India, Gandhi had to coin a new term, *satyagraha,* to symbolize his idea. In Japan, the traditional fusion of the concepts of peace and harmony greatly influ-enced the Japanese understanding of Gandhian ideas and this impor-tant theme will be taken up later in the paper.

Yet another possibility for the continuation of the term "nonresist-ance" was the censorship policy of prewar Japan. The desire of the authorities to avert internal unrest probably implied a preference for "nonresistance" because this would eliminate the antistate image of Gandhi. For example, while Tomotaro Yohena, writing in 1922, was allowed to mention Gandhi's civil disobedience movement against "British imperialism," he had nevertheless to be satisfied with the many passages blue-penciled by the censor. In fact, one extract from Thoreau on civil disobedience completely disappeared.[11]

At any rate, with the passage of time there came an improvement in the Japanese understanding of Gandhi. For some, nonresistance no longer seemed the appropriate term to characterize Gandhism. For instance, Murobuse admitted in 1933 that there seemed to him to be a contradiction between the impression created by the term "direct action" and that created by the term "mahatma." For Murobuse, the latter term seemed to be connected with *ahimsā*, the cardinal principle of Gandhism, while the former seemed rather reminiscent of Georges Sorel's "ethics of violence."[12]

It would not be fair to state that the prewar Japanese image of Gandhi was represented by reference to the posture of nonresistance alone. Certain Japanese writers emphasised the militant aspects of Gandhian political actions. One such writer was Kazunobu Kanokogi, author of *Gandhi and Satygraha,* published in 1922.[13] Identifying egoism and capitalism with the world domination of the Anglo-Saxon race, he thought that the purpose of world revolution should be the destruction of egoism, modern capitalism, Anglo-Saxon imperialism, and white supremacy.[14] Kanokogi completely overlooked the universalistic element in Gandhism and made Gandhi a racist.

Yet another scholar who emphasized the political importance of Gandhi's militant activities was Shūmei Ōkawa, who had studied Sanskrit at Tokyo Imperial University. In his book, *Makers of Asia* (1941) he was severely critical of the stereotyped Japanese image of Gandhi, pointing out that it had merely focused on his spiritual aspects.[15] For Ōkawa, the most important aspect of Gandhism was its resistance to British rule. He went on to say, "Whether the fight is carried on by strength of arms or by strength of soul, when we consider political movements this is not an essential problem at all." In this case, evidently he considered these as alternative strategies whereas in Gandhism the means and ends are inseparable.

II

The emphasis on Gandhian militancy also produced yet another misunderstanding among Japanese writers on this subject. These writers found in Gandhian teaching a revolutionary element and some compared him to Lenin (e.g., Kanokogi and Ōkawa). For some Gandhi was an "Indian revolutionary." Here, what the Japanese meant was rather significant. For Kanokogi, "Indian" meant colored people versus whites and the pure, spiritual and idealistic versus the egoistic, materialistic, and capitalistic. For Ōkawa, however, "Indian" meant the selection of an appropriate strategy to suit Indian traditions. "The Indian tradition" in this case, was characterized by adherence to spiritual principles which rejected the secular world.[16] By considering Gandhi's nonviolent strategy as merely a tactic designed to suit an Indian situation, Ōkawa (and, by a different analysis, Kanokogi) overlooked the universalistic characteristics to be found in Gandhi's teachings, characteristics which, though deeply embedded in a rich Indian tradition, nevertheless went far beyond this by incorporating universal elements. This alone, perhaps, explains the secret of his influence on such men as Martin Luther King, Jr., operating in a different era and a different culture.

As understood by Kanokogi, by perceiving the "revolutionary" characteristic to be found in Gandhi as indicating a racial revolutionary, Gandhi's method became particularistic. On the other hand, Ōkawa perceived Gandhi as representing a revolutionary in the sense that Gandhi had successfully mobilized the Indian masses against Western imperialism. But given that Ōkawa did not consider nonviolence as an essential factor, he later came to hold a greater esteem for the Subhas Chandra Bose. Writing in 1943, at a time when Bose had come to Japan, Ōkawa, wrote that nonviolent means were insufficient and that Mr. Bose, a man worthy of the title, "Sword of India," would understand Japan, "the Sword of Asia," fighting for Asian liberation, better than would any other Indian nationalist.[17]

Yonejirō Noguchi was yet another important figure who emphasized the militant element in Gandhian teaching. Early in 1943 he had this to say: "Nothing could be more wrong than to understand the *satygrapha* movement as quietistic resistance because of its relation to nonviolence. Gandhi is the heroic incarnation of resistance *per se*."[18] Noguchi differed from Ōkawa in that the latter's interpretation of Gandhian militancy rested on a political assessment while the former's assessment rested on religious grounds. Noguchi found in Gandhi an element of the "primitive spirit" which could confront the "egoistic and materialistic knowledge" of the West, and Britain in particular.[19]

Despite the differing interpretations, one common feature in all the ultranationalist views on India in general and Gandhi in particular, was the assumption that since Japan was fighting against Western imperialism, India and Gandhi ought to recognize Japan as the leader of Asia. This was wishful thinking.

Rabindranath Tagore, in his first visit to Japan in 1916 criticized the Japanese path to modernization. He distinguished clearly between Westernization and modernization and stated that Japan was merely imitating Western nationalism under the banner of "survival of the fittest." When Noguchi visited Gandhi in 1935, on being asked if he had a message for the Japanese people, Gandhi merely stated that everything he wanted to say had been said by Tagore earlier in the century.[20]

Despite these early indications that Indian leaders were not committed to Japan's vision of Asia, Japan entered into a war with China in 1937. Tagore responded with a fierce denunciation of Japan's actions and broke off relations with Noguchi. The latter, however, either could not, or would not understand Tagore or Gandhi over this matter. He wrote letters to the two men, emphasizing that this "holy war" was justified. At the same time, he sent an open letter to thirteen leading Indian newspapers. Tagore responded to the letter by expressing his great surprise (and dismay) and emphasizing the importance of friendly relations between China and Japan based on humanitarian principles. Noguchi, alas, simply reiterated that the sole purpose of waging such a war was to establish the Greater East Asia Coprosperity Sphere in order to destroy Western imperialism in Asia. He failed to understand, or simply did not wish to understand, that the Japanese war against China was considered by Tagore and Gandhi as by nature the same kind of aggression as that carried out by the Western imperialist powers.

In wartime Japan, a widespread idealized interpretation of the war existed, and since this was a "war for greater Asia" (*Daitōa Sensō*) all Asian countries would and should cooperate in the struggle. By "Asian," two things were meant: (1) the war was being fought against Western imperialism, which had oppressed the nations of Asia, therefore all Asian nations should unite under Japanese leadership; (2) by virtue of their geographical position alone, all Asian nations shared common values, culture and social systems with Japan, rather than with the Western powers.

One famous advocate of "greater Asianism," Yoshitarō Hirano, a former Marxist, wrote that Gandhi should be able to understand Japan far better than the other "liberal, democratic" leaders of the Indian nationalist movement because Gandhi was more "Oriental." To Hirano "Oriental" meant that "Gandhi stood apart from Western democracy" and that "he had no sympathy with majority rule and representation" because he was a product of Indian agrarian society.[21] In Japan, at this time, there was a strong antipathy towards Western democracy and liberalism and this antipathy was a powerful weapon in the anti-Western campaign within Japan. Thus, one can say that the above distorted interpretation of Gandhi was probably the result of a psychological projection of this antipathy.

One famous biographer of Gandhi, Tokumatsu Sakamoto, wrote in 1944, "The extension of the spirit of family to state and nation is an elemental Oriental spirit found in Gandhi and it is also the principle of Oriental political systems."[22] It is true that Gandhi did emphasize the importance of familial love as the prototype for universal brotherhood. However, it is important that one distinguishes between this and the family state in Japan where the state was considered an extended family with the Emperor at its head. The latter, in essence hierarchical, is in complete contrast with the idea of Gandhi that the "emphasis was consistently on the equality of members" in society.[23] Again, the use of "Oriental spirit" to characterize Gandhi, without severe qualifications, reflected the prevailing sociopsychological atmosphere of wartime Japan, rather than reality.

Despite a pervasive wishful thinking on the part of the Japanese that Gandhi and India would support their "mission," Gandhi clearly stated in *Harijan* on July 26, 1942, in an article entitled "To every Japanese"

> Our movement demanding the withdrawal of the British power from India should in no way be misunderstood. In fact, if we are to believe

your reported anxiety for the independence of India, a recognition of that independence by British should leave you no excuse for any attack on India. Moreover the reported profession sorts ill with your ruthless aggression against China.

I would ask you to make no mistake about the fact that you will be sadly disillusioned if you believe that you will receive a willing welcome from India. The end and aim of the movement for British withdrawal is to prepare India, by making her free for resisting all militarist and imperialist ambition, whether it is called British Imperialism, German Nazism, or your pattern.[24]

Although not widely known in Japan, Gandhi's attitude towards Japan eventually brought about a reevaluation of his teachings, role and importance. Noguchi, who had always emphasized the militant side of Gandhi now began to use the term "nonresistance" in 1942.[25] Expressing his dissatisfaction with Gandhi, Noguchi stated that nonviolent or "gradualist" means were insufficient for achieving Indian independence. He even went so far as to suggest that Gandhi retire from the political field because of these limitations.[26]

III

Japan's defeat in 1945 destroyed the Japanese Empire and the idea of a Greater East Asia Co-prosperity Sphere. Since then, there has been a remarkable growth of detached research on India. In addition to the long and distinguished tradition in Japan of the study of the Indian classics and early Buddhism, there has also emerged a more scientific study of modern and contemporary India. This has influenced both the academic world and Japan's wide reading public. As a result, an image of Gandhi much more accurate than hitherto has appeared. But in the popular mind there is still no positive image of India which can compare with the prewar image. On the one hand, the older generation and the Buddhists have a vaguely defined sympathy with India as the birth place of Buddhism. On the other, the younger generation and the more secular-minded usually adhere to a view deeply influenced by the stereotyped distinction between developed and developing countries.

At one point Nehru was very popular among Japanese as the leader of a neutralist policy but the evaluation was considerably influenced by political considerations: until the early 1950's, according to the communist view, only the socialist camp was considered to be peace-loving. On the other side was the capitalist camp, considered to be imperialist. In this conceptual framework there was no room for a third group of neutralist countries. Later, at the Bandung Conference in

1955, the communists came to rate Nehru's position highly. The political assessment of India underwent an abrupt change after the Sino-Indian dispute in 1962. Pro-Chinese leftists now came to view India as pro-American while conservative Japanese politicians utilized the dispute to show the inadequacy of a neutralist policy in the modern world and saw this as a basis for justifying a move to strengthen the existing Japanese Self-Defense Forces.

In addition to various changes in the views of India held by the Japanese, there has been another view, more stable and more deep-rooted, which while not often associated with Gandhian teaching directly, has considerable significance here. Gandhi wrote about the A-bomb in an article in *Harijan* on July 7, 1946: "The moral to be legitimately drawn from the supreme tragedy of the bomb is that it will not be destroyed by counterbombs even as violence cannot be by counterviolence. Mankind has to get out of violence by nonviolence."[27]

After having experienced the trauma of defeat in war, Japan renounced all war in Article 9 of its new Constitution in 1947. Having experienced also the trauma of the atomic bombing, the Japanese have become even more sensitive to the problems of war and peace in general and the danger of nuclear armaments in particular. In this sense, the Japanese are drawing on the moral mentioned by Gandhi. The Japanese popular attitude to war is exemplified by the results of opinion polls; for example, in 1965, 49 percent of all those interviewed opposed the American bombing of North Vietnam against only 14 percent who supported it. Public opinion also seems strongly against any form of nuclear testing by any country.

Despite the fact that such feelings are widespread and deeply rooted, they have not crystallized into absolute pacifism. Here the traditional fusion of the concepts of peace and harmony present a formidable barrier to the achievement of pacifism. Many Japanese, while interested in maintaining peace, prefer also to support harmony in the existing order, and therefore find it very difficult to "fight" for peace. In part, this dilemma was responsible for the political inactivity of so many Japanese in the 1930s and their failure to oppose the policy of aggressive war despite a long tradition of peace-loving Buddhist philosophy. For most people, the most important thing was to adhere to national conformity and not disturb social harmony, the inevitable result being that very few indeed resisted the war effort. Indeed, perceiving their social peace threatened by an external "enemy" they showed their concern by attempting to protect it in a ferocious war. Thus they adopted a standard of morality extremely different from the one applied to the preservation of internal harmony.[28]

This fusion between the concepts of peace and harmony often leads to a pronounced lack of criticism of the established order in Japan, producing an attitude of harmony-at-any-price which will tolerate any injustice, even war. In part, this fusion is responsible for the Japanese interpretation of Gandhian nonviolence as nonresistance.

There are some Japanese, though still few in number, who do advocate the principle of direct, nonviolent action. A good example of this is the Buddhist sect, Nihonzan Nyōhōji, led by Nittatsu Fujii. It is interesting to note that Fujii actually stayed at Gandhi's *ashram*. Indeed, such was his impression on Gandhi that later, when Gandhi was discussing his admiration for Japan, he expressly mentioned this monk.[29]

Leaving aside such movements directly influenced by Gandhi, there exists in Japan a broader social basis for a greater acceptance of Gandhi's teachings. One advantage for Japan in this respect is the existence of the "peace Constitution"; another is the fact that public opinion strongly opposes all wars and armaments.

Japan experienced rapid economic growth in the 1960s and this resulted in both an increased national confidence and a more conservative outlook. Thus, in many respects the Japanese situation now seems to have become less appropriate for the introduction of Gandhian ideas. The increasingly prevalent conservative mood, however, includes two different tendencies. The first is a pronounced decrease in antiwar feelings and a fading of the bad memories of World War II. The second is an even greater increase in maintaining a peaceful daily life. The former tendency is best indicated by the decrease in the number of protest movements against the continuing militarization. However, the latter trend may cancel out the former, in that an increased interest in maintaining a peaceful daily life means opposition to any radical change including a radical increase in Japan's military forces.

However, what is perhaps even more important is that in a mass post-industrial society like Japan, there has been not only "the end of ideology" but also the end of ideologies. Thus, a special effort is now, more than ever, needed to strengthen the belief in ideas, including pacifism. What is urgently needed is a decision as to where the effort should be directed. For the Japanese people, Gandhi, by his teachings and his actions, can provide considerable help in deciding that direction.

Notes

1. Taketane Takata, *Seiyū Gandhi*, Ōsakayagō Shoten, 1922.
2. Romain Rolland, *Seiyū Gandhi*, translated into Japanese by Masakiyo Miyamoto, Tōwashuppansha, 1942.
3. Yonejirō Noguchi, *Seiyū Gandhi*, Chōbunkaku, 1943. Noguchi visited India several times and lived with Tagore at his university at Santiniketan and translated many of Tagore's poems into Japanese.
4. Taketane Takata, *op. cit.*, p. ii.
5. Tadashi Shigemori, *Gandhi oyobi Gandhism*, Nihonhyōronsha, 1922, p. 6.
6. Takanobu Murobuse, *Mahatma Gandhi no Shisō to Undō*, Tōyōkyōkai, 1933, p. 34.
7. Riichiro Hoashi, *Tolstoy to Gandhi no Shūkyōshisō*. Keiseisha, 1922.
8. Tadashi Shigemori, *op. cit.*, p. 17,
9. Joan V. Bondurant, *Conquest of Violence, The Gandhian Philosophy of Conflict*, University of California Press, 1965, p. 186.
10. R. Hoashi, *op. cit.*, p. 96. Kan Fukunaga's introduction to the Japanese translation of C.F. Andrews, *Gandhi no Kakumei Undō to Shūkyō*, Taihōkaku, 1930, p. iv.
11. Tomotaro Yohena, "Shinri no Haji to Gandhi no Undō," *Kaizō*, April 1922.
12. Takanobu Murobuse, *op. cit.*, p. 32,
13. Kazunobu Kanokogi, *Gandhi to Shinri no Haji*, Kaizōsha, 1922.
14. *Ibid.*, pp. 348–351.
15. Shūmei Ōkawa, *Asia Kensetsusha*, Daiichishobō, 1941, p. 327.
16. S. Ōkawa, *Nihonteki Genkō*, Kōchisha, 1930; *Ōkawa Shumei Zenshu*, vol. 1, Okawa Shumei Zenshu Kankokai, 1961, p. 387.
17. S. Ōkawa, *Zenshu*, vol. 2, 1962, p. 916.
18. Y. Noguchi, *op. cit.*, p. 183.
19. *Ibid.*, p. 20
20. *Ibit.*, p. 156.
21. Yoshitarō Hirano, "Indo Dokuritsu Undō to Jūkei Seiken," *Kaizō*, September, 1943, p. 92.
22. Tokumatsu Sakamoto, *Gandhi*, Nihonhyōronsha, 1944, p. 106.
23. J. Bondurant, *op. cit.*, p. 161.
24. M.K. Gandhi, *Non-Violence in Peace and War*, vol. 1, 3rd ed., Navajivan Publishing House, Ahmedabad, 1948, pp. 408–409. *Harijan* was a weekly journal originally published in 1933 by Gandhi to promote his movement. It sometimes stopped publishing because of the political situation but survived more than ten years.
25. Y. Noguchi, *Tateyo Indo*, Shōgakkan, 1942, p. 228.
26. *Ibid.*, p. 46.
27. M.K. Gandhi, *op. cit.*, vol. 2, 1949, p. 97.
28. For more detail see chapter six.
29. M.K. Gandhi, *op. cit.*, vol. 1, p. 408.

CHAPTER EIGHT

The Significance of Nonviolent Direct Action: A Japanese Perspective

I

In recent years the term "peace research" has become increasingly widespread, both abroad and in Japan. However, precisely what is meant by this term is not always clear. Problems of definition apart, what is clear is that peace research, due to the widespread assertion that it must be multidisciplinary in method, is something rather different from research in a single discipline. Peace research can only be defined in terms of its goal, namely peace. Of course, if one understands peace research as something oriented towards that particular goal, certain problems inevitably occur. For example, there is the general problem of how to deal with value judgements in social science research. Yet another problem is whether one can define the value of peace without ambiguity. Regardless of whether a researcher admits it or not, all social scientific research has its own value premises. Max Weber and Karl Mannheim have proposed that the bias stemming from such value premises may be avoided by being aware of the premises and by reflecting on them. In the more recent "postbehavioral revolution" the importance of the need to reflect on one's value premises has been stressed by David Easton.[1] Peace research, in fact, represents a rather extreme example of this general problem area. Reflection on one's value premises, in order to maintain objectivity, is a vital part of the social sciences in general and peace research in particular.

The ambiguity inherent in the term produces even greater difficulties.[2] On the one hand, in a negative sense, peace can be defined as the lack of physical violence. On the other hand, in a positive sense, the same term may be applied to the necessity for social change on behalf

147

of such positive values as, equality, social justice, and prosperity. In the former, peace means the maintenance of the status quo, in the latter, peace tends to oppose the existing order. The first might well be called peace-keeping and the second peace-building. The end result here is that peace can have different and even opposite meanings.

The crucial problem today is how to eradicate injustice in the world without causing physical violence. Social change, including change in the international order, through nonviolent means, would seem to offer the only possible solution to this problem. Such a conclusion however, is merely theoretical; whether such a solution is practical will be discussed later. Before dealing with the practicality of nonviolent direct action, a review of the development of peace research may provide hints as to an appropriate approach.

Historically, peace research developed naturally out of studies concerning war between states, due to the fact that such war has been a legitimate use of violence on a massive scale. The motive behind such peace research was the avoidance of physical conflict between states. Such an approach had obvious limitations in that, even if a way was found to avoid conflict between states, whether such states would choose to adopt such a policy was quite another matter. In this context, an important principle proposed by Kant concerning the close relationship between international peace and domestic political structure ought to be borne in mind. Kant stated clearly that in order to maintain international peace, it was necessary that each state have a democratic political system.[3]

The next step in peace research was the trend towards dealing with internal political situations *in addition* to the international order. In the case of simulation, for example, a sovereign state is no longer considered as a single actor but the various forces within the state are the actors. In this way, it is possible to predict more precisely than before what will happen if each actor behaves in a certain way. Nevertheless, the problem remains as to how one can force each political actor to behave in such a way as to avoid international war. In other words, how can the ordinary citizen, alienated from the political elites, alter the decision making process.

Today, a problem which is particularly serious is that democratic government has been able to maintain law and order but has failed to abolish injustice within states, and war with other countries. There is a tendency today for people to state that parliamentary democracy is not sufficient in order to abolish injustice and war, citing as examples racial conflict in the United States and the Vietnam War. If a way out of such a situation is to be found, it is vital that whatever drastic method of change is chosen, it must not destroy the democratic order. Such a change requires conflict but, if the conflict is physical, it can easily lead to anarchy. Joan Bondurant, attempting to apply Mahatma Gandhi's philosophy to the contemporary American situation, concluded that "a careful analysis of the dynamics of *satyagraha* points the direction in which liberal democratic thought could be advanced." Thus she provided a thoughtful answer to the questions, "How can conflict be constructed constructively?" and "How can man engage in conflict without the danger of annihilation?"[4] The present political situation makes the problem of nonviolent direct action an urgent one and points out the importance of solving the ambivalence inherent in the term "peace."

Given the importance of nonviolent direct action, the question remains as to how to deal with it as a subject for peace research. Until now, a limited number of approaches to this problem have been attempted. One such approach has been the religious, philosophical, or moral approach. This developed earliest due to nonviolent action emerging as a religious phenomenon at the time of the Reformation and continues today in such sects as the Friends (Quakers). The provisions for conscientous objectors are evidence of the efforts made utilizing this approach. The religious type of analysis is exemplified in Roland H. Bainton's *Christian Attitudes Toward War and Peace*.[5] The philosophical or moral approach to the nonviolent direct action can be found among some Indian disciples of Gandhi. All of these are important in order to show the religious or moral value of such action, but are insufficient in that they fail to show how it might effectively be used in a political context.

A second approach is the study of historical cases of nonviolent direct action. This approach often overlaps considerably with the first approach in that many case studies focus on action based on religious grounds. Some of the articles cited in Adam Roberts' *Civilian Resistance as a National Defense* represent examples of this approach.[6] Since historical acts cannot be recreated, careful investigation of the historical context is needed in order to indicate in what sense, and to what extent, such cases may be utilized for generalization.

The third approach is the technical one, exemplified by Gene Sharp's *Exploring Nonviolent Alternatives*.[7] Many textbooks reflecting this approach have been published by Quaker groups. This approach, while useful in training people in the use of nonviolent strategy, fails to indicate how effective such strategies will be in given situations, and needs to be supplemented by some means of analyzing the broader social context.

In order to overcome the shortcomings inherent in the above approaches, what is suggested here is the political approach. "Political" here might be interpreted rather narrowly as suggestive of an approach focusing on a specific nonviolent direct action and its political effects. In this chapter the term is used much more broadly. It indicates the analysis of relationships between goals, means, and effects in sociopolitical contexts. The effectiveness of nonviolent action ought to be investigated by considering particular circumstances such as socioeconomic conditions (such as whether the society is agrarian or postindustrial), the international situation (whether the society is colonized or independent) and the domestic political situation (such as how the democratic process operates). The nonviolent strategies of Gandhi and Martin Luther King can be correctly understood, in comparative terms, if the above circumstances are given due consideration.

How can this political approach to nonviolent direct action be developed? First, four aspects to be analyzed are offered: (1) the goal towards which the action is oriented (this includes not only rational goals but also emotive symbols), (2) the structure of the organization dedicated to the action, including the problem of leadership, (3) the concrete action chosen as a means of nonviolent strategy in a particular situation, and (4) the short and long-term political effects of such action. Rather than giving an extended theoretical explanation of these aspects, the method adopted here will be to utilize certain Japanese case studies as a means of demonstrating the practical significance of this approach. Since these cases are the product of Japanese situations, one cannot immediately draw universal generalizations. Modern Japan is a densely populated, highly industrialized, mass society. Its agrarian sector is rather different from that of other agrarian societies to which it has sometimes been compared, e.g., Chinese and Yugoslavian societies during World War II, where there were important peasant guerilla movements. In terms of international relations, Japan has never been colonized although it was subjected to military occupation after World War II and even today has many American military bases. If one bears these special characteristics in mind, overgeneralization can be avoided and the study of Japanese cases can be useful both for comparative purposes and for evolving a general theory of nonviolent direct action.

Brief mention must be made of the particular circumstances of Japan's wartime defeat and postwar Occupation. This is particularly true in the case of Okinawa, where the Occupation army after a fierce land battle, completely disarmed all the inhabitants and assumed total control, ignoring both the Japanese and American legal systems in the process. For example, the peasants of Iye island, one of the Okinawa chain, had recourse only to nonviolent direct action in order to bring about the removal of missile bases. This situation might well be considered analogous to the use of a strategy of civilian resistance, should Japan become an unarmed country and face military invasion in the future. Therefore, Japan's past experiences of nonviolent direct action can provide us not only with cases concerning domestic decision making (particularly in relation to the U.S.-Japan security treaty), but also with examples which can be of use in mapping out strategies of civilian resistance.

II

In Japan the goal underlying mass protests for peace has often been a combination of two forces: a widespread antiwar sentiment and the people's interest in maintaining a peaceful daily life, particularly in rural areas where, in a densely populated country, the attachment to landed property is very strong. The first example of this kind was the Uchinada case, which began in 1953. Uchinada was a village located in Ishikawa prefecture on the Japan Sea; its principal industries were farming and fishing. A serious protest took place when the government decided to use the village land for artillery testing. The major slogans in the campaign against the government were "Compensation money is temporary, land is forever" and "Let us not lose the land where the graves of our ancestors are located." A widespread fear of Japan's possible involvement in war because of the Cold War situation gave added strength to their cause. The villagers' movement received wide support from leftist forces, particularly the General Council of Trade Unions of Japan (Sōhyō), and from intellectuals. However, the peasants' preoccupation with their own daily lives had ambivalent effects: on the one hand, it was the real motivation underlying their protest and on the other hand, it caused some of the villagers to abandon the movement on the grounds that it was being manipulated by alarmists from outside. The latter group reasoned that it would be better for them to reconstruct the village by their own efforts, using compensation funds. Those who abandoned the protest movement organized a group called *Aisondōshikai* (literally, Brotherhood of Those Who Love the Village). They argued that "loving the village" was related to "loving the nation" and thus the necessity of national security justified the artillery tests.

The protest movement in Uchinada failed, but a similar case in Sunakawa brought a victory for the protestors. The case began when in

1955 the government decided to expropriate peasant land in Sunakawa in order to expand the American air base located there. The movement continued for fourteen years and the government finally abandoned its plan in 1968. Initially, the Sunakawa case, like the Uchinada case, had as its strongest motivation the peasants' interest in the land. In fact, the leader of the movement, a farmer who later became a radical activist, was astonished when, for the first time in his life, he saw red flags carried by union workers who had come to support the peasants. The goal of the movement gradually shifted from a particular interest to more general ones, such as the call for the abolition of American military bases and the condemnation of the U.S.-Japan security treaty. When the U.S. air force decided to leave the base, in 1969, the leaders of this movement shifted their protest to opposing the military use of the land by the Japanese Self-Defense Forces.

A similar change in goal can be seen in the movement protesting against the target range at Kitafuji, north of Mount Fuji. Here again, the movement was based on defense of land, in this case the peasants' rights to common land. One slogan, "Peasants are grass grown on the land," suggests the deep interest the peasants had in their land. As the movement developed however, more universalistic goals appeared, as seen in the slogan "Don't connect Mount Fuji with Vietnam!" In the same way as in the Sunakawa case, the peasants in this area then switched their protests to opposing the military use of that land by the Self-Defense Forces.

Such changes in goals are more rapid in urban areas. In 1968 a protest movement emerged opposing the American military field hospital in Ōji, located at the center of one of the most densely populated areas in the Tokyo metropolitan region. At first the people's major interests were the noise of helicopters carrying patients from Vietnam, the danger of contagious tropical deseases, the prostitution encouraged by the presence of GI's. The movement attracted much popular attention and gained wide support, finally attaining its objective when the hospital was removed.

Also in 1968, another protest movement against a field hospital was organized by intellectuals and citizens in Asaka. Here a "protest against the American invasion in Vietnam" was one of the initial goals of the movement in addition to the demands for the solution of noise and other problems resulting from the field hospital being located in that area. Activists even tried broadcasting over the hospital fence in an effort to persuade the GI patients to join the protest against the war in Vietnam. This kind of activity was in the direction of international solidarity for peace rather than nationalist sentiment against foreign military forces.

In 1972, a movement was launched to prevent American tanks being transported to Vietnam from a supply base at Sagamihara. In this case the problems of noise and interference in daily life were not the major issues. The most important slogan was "Don't connect Route 16 with Vietnam!" This movement attained some temporary success since it won the support of the socialist Mayor of Yokohama and because the tanks violated the weight limitations laid down by the Road Traffic Act. The government later revised the Road Traffic Act to allow special exceptions in the case of American military transport. The tanks were successfully transported and the police force moved in to remove protestors who sat down in front of the tanks.

These historical examples indicate a change in goals from the preservation of particular vested interests or the fear of involvement in war, to a more universal active pursuit of peace and to criticism against the government's policy of supporting the war in Vietnam. A similar progression may be seen in the development of the antinuclear movement. Initially, the Japanese people, as the first victims of the bomb, protested against it from the standpoint of victims. In 1949, American testing in the Pacific caused contamination of fish. The Japanese, being both particularly sensitive to the effects of radioactivity as well as great eaters of fish, felt that their daily life was being directly threatened. This naturally contributed to the strengthening of the movement. Ironically though, the victims of Hiroshima and Nagasaki were discriminated against by their fellow Japanese in terms of marriage and employment. It is only comparatively recently that compassion for the bomb victims has increased, along with an understanding for those affected by environmental disruption. A further extension is the concern for A-bomb victims of Korean nationality, a group which has been long neglected. An awareness has emerged that such Koreans have been the victims of both the A-bomb and of Japanese imperialism. In this way the focus has clearly changed from a sense of being threatened to a positive reflection on one's own involvement in wars, either past or present, and from a national to an international emphasis.

III

In Japan, in terms of organization, there was a historic shift in the role played by trade unions. The General Council of Trade Unions of Japan, in the late 1950s and early 1960s, played a decisive role in protests in both urban and rural areas. The General Council dispatched many workers to protest areas and this resulted in many of the movements becoming national issues. This provided local people with the opportunity of broadening the scope of their protests. At the same time, this outside mobilization caused many local people to feel that the situation was being utilized by alarmists for their own purposes. This feeling was particularly prevalent in rural areas and was perceived as merely making the negotiations more difficult. In Uchinada and elsewhere, local protesters interested solely in negotiation with the government brandished slogans such as "Go Home Strangers!" In certain cases where physical violence occurred between the police and protesters (especially radical students) local shopkeepers tended to oppose such protests on the grounds that "the peace of the town must be maintained."

This sort of mobilization from outside often produced impressive results in terms of the actual numbers participating but rarely lasted for more than a short period of time. Thus, if a movement is overly dependent on such outside support it will tend to decline rapidly. One further difficulty with such outside assistance is that, as was the case with the national federation of trade unions in the 1960s, there grows a feeling of distrust toward such organizations. Rapid economic development has tended to favor union members and usually organized workers have come from large scale industries, in contrast to the small industry sector where the workers have tended to be rather poorly organized. In addition, since Japanese unions are company-wide rather than organized by industries or by trades, the tendency toward corporate mergers has produced not only an economic oligopoly on the part of management but also a similar trend toward oligopoly in the unions themselves.

Even as early as 1960, when hundreds of thousands protested against the revised security treaty, there were clear signs that the national federation of trade unions had lost some of its earlier influence.[8] Instead, tiny "voluntary" groups such as the Group of the Voiceless Voices emerged and later came to play an important part in Japan's Peace in Vietnam Committee *(Beheiren);* this movement began in 1965 and was a result of protests against the bombing of North Vietnam. *Beheiren* organized monthly meetings and rallies but had no formal membership. Those who were interested in the cause could simply join on an *ad hoc* basis. The result was a sort of "organization without organization" which sought to avoid having a bureaucratic structure.

In 1968, when the nuclear powered carrier USS *Enterprise* entered Sasebo some union workers organized a protest movement in cooperation with some citizen groups. This act on the part of the workers was in opposition to the policy laid down by the national leadership. The result was the creation of an antimainstream group called the "antiwar faction," composed principally of young rank-and-file union members, and this group became the focal point for radical protest.

Clearly this was evidence of a growing antipathy towards large organizations and this phenomenon is also evident in the increased role in protest movements played by unorganized crowds. This phenomenon, particularly common in urban areas, resulted when many people, both concerned and simply curious, appearing at certain protest sites often without being asked. This was particularly true of the movements in the metropolitan area, such as the demonstrations at Ōji in 1968 and Sagamihara in 1972. While some came mainly out of a kind of mob spirit many others were half observer, half participant, sometimes in such techniques as "sit downs" and sometimes as victims or observers of the numerous examples of police brutality. The numbers of "half participants" has been growing over time.

In rural areas the situation has been rather different. At Kitafuji for example, despite occasional external support from workers and students, the villagers themselves pursued this type of protest for 27 years, from the beginning of the Allied Occupation. The protest movement here became deeply rooted in village life becoming a sort of *Schicksalsgemeinschaft* "community of common fate." The combination here of living together and protesting together and the face-to-face relationships and mutual aid techniques were of a sort which could not be found among city dwellers.

Sunakawa, although a farming village, was actually located in suburban Tokyo and the feeling of solidarity was less than at Kitafuji. In fact the protest there was organized on the basis of a federation of neighborhood associations. The area also had some factory workers and these played a linkage role between the farmers and the unions.

In Ōji, located in central Tokyo, the solidarity between shopkeepers in the same street played a similar role to that of neighborhood associations in the villages. Nevertheless, such solidarity among the old middle class has played an ambivalent role in the protest movement. At Ōji, the principal motive of the movement against the field hospital was the desire for the preservation of a stable and prosperous life. This same interest also led, at times, to opposition to the protest movement in that such activities themselves threatened the harmony of the community. The existence of a high concentration of workers in small industries located in this area also led to labor participating as activists in the movement or merely as part of the "mob."

If the Kitafuji case was typically rural, the protest movement at Sagamihara represents an excellent example of a typically urban situation. Sagamihara had few farmers and few members of the old middle class. In addition none of the residents in the area actually felt that their own personal interests were at stake. In fact, it was the antiwar element rather than any local interest which provided the driving force behind this protest movement. Despite the fact that an organization was formed by inhabitants of this area it was neither on behalf of, or limited to, local inhabitants.

This urban-rural cleavage is probably less acute in Japan than in many other countries since Japan is limited in area, densely populated, and possesses a highly developed communication and transport network. Rapid urbanization has contributed to the lessening of urban-rural differences. Nevertheless, special efforts have been made by some movement leaders to bridge the gap between the differences which still exist. For example, student activists who attempted to help the farmers tried to settle in the area and helped with their labor. In 1972, some 300 students were to be found doing this in Sanrizuka, where farmers were protesting against the construction of the new airport at Narita.

Thus far, the attention has focused on the protest movement as a whole; the specific organizations for nonviolent action have not been mentioned. This is because there are very few organizations dedicated specifically to nonviolent action and also because protest in Japan tends to be rather less violent than elsewhere, partly due to the tradition of an unarmed citizenry. The instances where Molotov cocktails and the like have been used are relatively rare. Rather, staves, stones, and "snake dances"—where the protesters weave through the streets causing massive traffic jams—have been the common armory of protesters. In the face of a well-equipped and extensive police machine, the avoidance of violent strategy is sensible and effective in that one can obtain a stronger moral position *vis-à-vis* police brutality and hence increase one's public support. Of course, theoretically, a clear distinction must be made between nonviolent and violent means no matter how minor the use of violence in use.[9]

Japan has failed to produce any great leaders of nonviolent direct action in the tradition of a Gandhi or a Martin Luther King. Religious leaders are conspicuous by their absence due in part to the fact that in modern Japan society has become highly secularized and religious activities are regarded as little more than rituals. One Buddhist sect, the Nihonzan Myōhōji has made a considerable impact as one of the very few organizations dedicated to nonviolent direct action. Monks of this sect, led by the Rev. Nittatsu Fujii, are often to be found in the vanguard of many nonviolent rallies, beating drums and uttering holy invocations. However, impressive as their presence is, their influence is limited by the smallness of this particular sect.

In fact, the most important organizations involved in nonviolent direct action may well be women's groups. In Kitafuji for example, the Shibokusa mother's organization, formed in 1960, played a decisive role in the protest movement there. Leaders of this group argued that it was natural that women should be in the vanguard of such movements leaving the men to the task of production. Yet another organization, composed mainly of younger women in their twenties and thirties, the Young Wives Association has emerged since 1970. It may well be that the leadership has intuitively sensed that women can better convey the concept of nonviolence and are even more effective in the face of police brutality. Similarly, groups composed of senior citizens, such as the Action Group for the Aged, have also appeared. In the protest against the airport at Sanrizuka, some 140 members of this particular group, along with the 360-member Women's Action Group have consistently occupied the front line of the protests there. Given the existence of violent and nonviolent activist in the same protest movement it is essential that the problem of identification be resolved and monks, women, and senior citizens have an additional advantage in this context.

IV

Finally, what have been the nonviolent techniques utilized by the Japanese in pursuit of their objectives? These vary, according to the situation but among the best examples are the following; sit-ins at target sites in order to obstruct artillery tests (Kitafuji); flying kites in the flightpaths in the vicinity of airbases (Sunakawa); smoke signals to obstruct artillery tests and transport flights (Kitafuji and Sunakawa); defiantly cultivating land threatened with confiscation (Kitafuji and Okinawa); and lying down on the road to prevent the transportation of tanks (Sagamihara). Generally speaking, the most effective strategy has been a skilful combination of legal actions such as law suits, and illegal but nonviolent direct action.[10] In Sunakawa, for example, the leader of the movement, a simple farmer, became so well versed in legal problems by virtue of the number of legal suits filed, that he is now referred to as Sunakawa's minister of justice. One such law suit achieved a momentous decision when the District Court ruled that the presence of American troops in Japan was unconstitutional, but this verdict was almost immediately reversed by the Supreme Court. In other cases, such as Kitafuji, law suits not only aided the strategic actions but also increased the farmers' awareness of their own rights.

In cases where a protest movement produces excitement among the members, it is always very difficult to adhere to a nonviolent strategy. As Japanese movements have lacked the charasmatic leadership of a Gandhi or a Martin Luther King, mutual agreement among members has often checked this danger. For example, in the Iye island case the villagers themselves decided not to put their hands higher than their ears so as not to appear to be threatening the American military personnel. This was particularly important because language barriers tend to create great misunderstandings. In the Asaka case too, the participants were advised to fold their arms in order to avoid confrontation with the police. In general, the more serious the situation, the more careful protestors have been in choosing appropriate means. In addition, those most directly concerned with the issue, usually the local population, tend to be more careful than students or workers coming in from outside. This is not necessarily due to farmers being more conservative, but simply because they have to consider long term effects as well as immediate results.

In a typical case, both violent and nonviolent actions coexist in the same movement. Thus it is often difficult to separate the effects of these two opposing strategies. There is some support for those who emphasise the effectiveness of violent action in that generally speaking it is the more violent actions (such as physical clashes between police and students) which tend to dominate media coverage. Nevertheless, such publicity has a double-edged effect in that, on the one hand it does attract attention and may increase popular intrest in the issue, but on the other hand, sympathy with the movement may decline because of the very violence used. In addition police authorities can gain support for their appeals for more and stronger equipment.

It would be quite premature and improper to construct any definite theory on the basis of such a small number of scattered cases. However, the author believes that an investigation of many more concrete cases, in terms of an analysis of the relationships between goals, means, and effects is worthy of extended investigation. Only an accumulation of this kind of evidence can provide us with guidelines as to how nonviolent direct action, at a practical level, can succeed in a given set of circumstances. A comparison of similar cases in other societies might well provide the means for establishing a general theory, and this essay is hopefully a first tentative step in that direction.

Postscript

Since the termination of the war in Vietnam, the widespread fear among Japanese that they might be directly involved in a war has been gradually diminishing. Mass protests against war are no longer commonplace. Moreover, as memories of World War II have become more and more remote, and a new generation with no experience of World War II has emerged, antiwar sentiment in general has been declining. Also, rapid economic growth during the 1960s and early 1970s has resulted in an increased sense of national confidence in one way or another.

The above change in the general attitude of Japanese people towards war has made the policy of nonviolent direct action against war much less conspicuous than before. However, a similar nonviolent strategy is still being used by antipollution and other citizens' movements. Much of this is related to the problem of peace in a broader sense. For instance, the movement against atomic power stations in Japan has a close link with the Japanese people's feeling about the A-bomb. This is often labeled "the nuclear allergy" by those who are in favor of atomic energy. Antipollution movements, too, by questioning the Japanese pattern of rapid development have tried to attract popular attention to the basic problem of creating a suitable environment for human existence. They are attempting to shift the popular emphasis from wealth to welfare.

Despite changes in the domestic situation since this essay was written in 1971, the problem of nonviolent direct action is still important for peace-building within Japan. If we look at the international situation, however, the U.S. government is constantly pressuring Japan to increase armaments, which were originally prohibited by the American occupation authorities. Domestically, too, with the general increase in national confidence, there is an increasing call for the strengthening of Japan's euphemistically named Self-Defense Forces. Japanese pacifists are facing considerable difficulties in that they are expected to provide proof that nonviolent direct action is sufficient for effective self-defense. Certainly the historical record offers little support for the pacifist position, but proponents of increased armaments are not expected to provide evidence that *their* policies are effective for self-defense. In their case too, the historical record offers little support. It is hardly fair to ask categorically whether nonviolent means can perfectly guarantee a nation's security, since the question is really, which is safer in a relative sense. In other words, the choice should be between an increase in armament which may result in an escalation of the arms race, and the decrease or abolition of existing armament. The latter will naturally result in weakening of physical force but may also result in a de-escalation in the arms race. The effectiveness of nonviolent direct action as a means for defending a nation is a problem for the future. This is because there are not enough adequate historical examples on which to base policy. In addition, the effectiveness depends on the strength of the people's belief in pacifism, which has not yet fully matured. The principal duty of peace researchers must be to continue to investigate various cases, in both a specific and comparative context, in order to build a general theory for the effective application of nonviolent direct action.

Notes

1. David Easton, "The New Revolution in Political Science," *American Political Science Review*, vol. 63, no. 4, Dec. 1969.
2. For the various meanings of "peace" in different cultures, see chapter six.
3. Immanuel Kant, *Zum ewigen Frieden, ein philosophischer Entwurf*, 1795. Kant used the term *republikanisch*, which literally means "republican," but which he understood to mean "democratic" or "constitutional".
4. Joan V. Bondurant, *Conquest of Violence, the Gandhian Philosophy of Conflict*, University of California Press, 1965, pp. x–xi.
5. Roland H. Bainton, *Christian Attitudes toward War and Peace*, New York, Abingdon Press, 1960.
6. Adam Roberts (ed.), *Civilian Resistance as a National Defence*, Pelican, 1969.
7. Gene Sharp, *Exploring Nonviolent Alternatives*, Boston, Porter Sargent, 1970.
8. For the varieties of participants in this movement, see George Packard III, *Protest in Tokyo, the Security Treaty of 1960*, Princeton University Press, 1966.
9. I clearly stated the necessity of distinguishing between violent and nonviolent means in my *Heiwa no Seijigaku* (*Politics for Peace*, Iwanami, Tokyo, 1968), arguing as follows. Violence in my definition is an action which either actually or potentially causes physical injury and does not encompass damage of property since the latter can be compensated by financial means. This distinction thus sees violence as causing physical injury, such as death or deformation, which cannot be recovered by *any* means. It must also be stressed that even if the violence is of a very low level at the beginning, it quickly tends to escalate.
10. "Nonviolent direct action" does not exclude illegal actions. According to my definition, nonviolent direct action means nonviolent action which exerts direct political influence without using a representative system. This may include "illegal" actions, depending on the existing legal system. For instance, those who sit down in the street to stop tanks, a completely nonviolent act, may well be prosecuted for violating the Road Transportation Act.

Bibliography of Takeshi Ishida

1954

Meiji Seiji Shisōshi Kenkyū (Studies in the History of Meiji Political Thought), Tokyo, Miraisha.

1956

Kindai Nihon Seijikōzō no Kenkyū (Studies in the Political Structure of Modern Japan), Tokyo, Miraisha.

1960

"The Diet Majority and Public Opinion," *Far Eastern Survey*, vol. 29, no. 10, (Oct.).

1961

Gendai Soshikiron (Contemporary Organization), Tokyo, Iwanami Shoten.

1962

Sengo Nihon no Seijitaisei (The Political System in Postwar Japan), Tokyo, Miraisha.
"Popular Attitudes toward the Japanese Emperor," *Asian Survey*, vol. 2, no. 2, (April).

1965

"Movements to Protect Constitutional Government - A Structural-Functional Analysis," translated and summarized from *Kindai Nihon Seiji Kōzō no Kenkyū* by George O. Totten, Totten(ed.), *Democracy in Prewar Japan*, Boston, Heath.

1966

*"A Current Japanese Interpretation of Max Weber," *The Developing Economies*, Tokyo, Institute of Asian Economic Affairs, vol. 4, no. 3. (Sept.).

1967

"Urbanization and Its Impact on Japanese Politics—The Case of a Late and Rapidly Developed Country," *Annals of the Institute of Social Science,* University of Tokyo, no. 8.

"Japanese Public Opinion and Foreign Policy—Present Aspects and Future Outlook," *Peace Research in Japan, 1967,* Japan Peace Research Group.

1968

Heiwa no Seijigaku (Politics for Peace), Tokyo, Iwanami Shoten.

Hakyoku to Heiwa: 1941-1952 (Catastrophe and Peace: Analysis of the Political Process in Japan 1941-1952), University of Tokyo Press.

"The Assimilation of Western Political Ideas and the Modernization of Japan," *Fukuoka UNESCO,* Fukuoka UNESCO Association, no. 4 (Oct.).

"Emerging or Eclipsing Citizenship?—A Study of Changes in Political Attitudes in Postwar Japan," *The Developing Economies,* vol. 6, no. 4. (Dec.).

"The Development of Interest Groups and the Pattern of Political Modernization in Japan," Robert E. Ward (ed.), *Political Development in Modern Japan,* Princeton University Press.

"The Education and Recruitment of Governing Elites in Modern Japan," Rupert Wilkinson (ed.), *Governing Elites: Studies in Training and Selection,* New York, Oxford University Press, co-authored with Yoshinori Ide.

1969

Seiji to Bunka (Politics and Culture), University of Tokyo Press.

"L'échec, effet de la réussite," *Les Temps Modernes,* no. 272 (Fevrier).

*"Beyond the Traditional Concepts of Peace in Different Cultures," *Journal of Peace Research,* Oslo, Peace Research Institute, no. 5.

*"Japan's Changing Image of Gandhi," *Peace Research in Japan, 1969.*

1970

Nihon no Seijibunka: Dōchō to Kyōsō (Japan's Political Culture: Conformity and Competition), University of Tokyo Press.

"Changing Society and Peace Research," *Peace Research in Japan, 1970.*

1971

Japanese Society, New York, Random House, 1971.

"A Content Analysis of Chief Justice of the Supreme Court Kotaro Tanaka's Speeches," *Annals of the Institute of Social Science,* University of Tokyo, no. 12.

"Japón Actual, Opinión pública y politica de Gobierno," *Estudio Orientales,* El Colegio de Mexico, vol. 6, no. 3.

1972

Mehiko to Nihonjin: Daisan Sekai de Kangaeru (Mexico and the Japanese: Observations from the Third World), Tokyo, University of Tokyo Press.

*"The Significance of Non-Violent Direct Action—As Viewed by a Japanese Political Scientist," *Peace Research in Japan,* 1972.

"Conformismo y Competencia en la Sociedad Japonesa," *Revista de la Universidad,* Universidad Nacional Autónoma de México, no. 6–8, 1972.

1973

Heiwa to Henkaku no Ronri (The Logic of Peace and Social Change), Tokyo, Renga Shobō.

"Peace Activities and Peace Research," *Peace Research in Japan, 1973.*

1974

"Interest Groups under a Semipermanent Government Party: the Case of Japan," *The Annals of the American Academy of Political and Social Science* (May).

"Can a Late-Developing Area Achieve a Better Quality of Life by 'Catching Up' with a Developed Area?" *Peace Research in Japan, 1974.*

1975

"Fundamental Human Rights and the Development of Legal Thought in Japan," translated by Hiroshi Wagatsuma and Beverly Braverman, *Law in Japan,* Japanese American Society for Legal Studies, vol. 8.

1976

Kindai Nihon Shisōshi ni okeru Hō to Seiji (Law and Politics in the History of Modern Japanese Thought), Tokyo, Iwanami Shoten.

*"Elements of Tradition and 'Renovation' in Japan during the 'Era of

Fascism'," *Annals of the Institute of Social Science,* University of Tokyo, no. 17.

1978

Gendai Seiji no Soshiki to Shōchō: Sengoshi eno Seijigakuteki Sekkin (Organizations and Symbols in Contemporary Politics, A Political Scientist's View of Postwar Japan).
"Cultural Contacts and the New Style of Thinking: The Case of Fukuzawa Yukichi," *Annals of the Institute of Social Science,* no. 19.

1980

*Combination of Conformity and Competition: A Key to Understand Japanese Society, Tokyo, Foreign Press Center.
"The Experience of Japanese Modernization: An Evaluation", (a paper presented at "The International Symposium on Islamic Civilization and Japan", sponsored by the Japan Foundation, held at Tokyo in March 1980).

1981

"The Significance of Intercultural Dialogue," *Bulletin of Peace Proposal,* Universitets fortaget, vol. 12, no. 2.
*"Westernism and Western 'Isms' in Modern Japan," *History of European Ideas,* vol. 1, no. 4.
"A Look at the New China," *Japan Echo,* vol. 8, special issue, 1981.
Shuhen kara no Shikō (Reflections from the Periphery), Tokyo, Tabata Shoten.
"The Meaning of 'Independence' in the Thought of Uchimura Kanzō," Ray A. Moore (ed.), *Culture and Religion in Japanese-American Relations: Essays on Uchimura Kanzō,* Michigan Papers in Japanese Studies, no. 5, Ann Arbor, University of Michigan.
"Nōkyō: the Japanese Farmers' Representatiave," Peter Drysdale et al. (eds.), *Japan and Australia: Two Societies and their Interrelation,* Canberra, Australian National University Press, co-authored with Auralia D. George.

1982

"Cultural and Religious Tradition and Human Rights in Japan," *Annals of the Institute of Social Science,* no. 23.
"Some Characteristics of Political Science in Japan," *Government and Opposition,* vol. 17, no. 3.
"Staat und Gesellschaft im modernen Japan in Zusammenhang mit der Entwickelung der Sozialwissenschaften," *Occasional Paper,* no. 20, Ostasiatisches Seminar, Freie Universität, Berlin.

Forthcoming

"Conflict and Conflict Accommodation in Japan: Viewed in Terms of *Omote-Ura* und *Uchi-Soto* Relations," Ellis Krauss et al. (eds.), *Conflict in Japan.*
*Revised version included in this volume.

Index

A-bomb, Gandhi's view of, 144; Korean victims of, 153; and opposition to nuclear power, 159; survivors, 128

Ahiṁsā, aspect of peace in, 119-23

Agricultural cooperatives, 16, 22 n; comparison with prewar organizations, 111

Aikokusha, forerunner of Jiyūtō, 71

Amae, Doi's idea of, 108-9

Anarchists and labor movement, 79

Anomie in Germany, 104

Antitrust regulations eased, 33

Anxiety and 1929 economic crisis, 81

Apathy: and affluence, 133; in large organizations, 43; in mass society, 91, 131; as passive obedience, 130; as reaction to mass education, 76

Armament and Western superiority, 69

Armed forces. *See* Self-Defense Forces

Assassination: of Premier Inukai, 98; February 26, 1936 incident, 32

Association for Service to the State through Industry, 97

Bell, Daniel, "end of ideology" phenomenon, 59

Bellah, Robert N., 64, 68 n

Bendix, Reinhard, on Japanese and German homogeneity, 53, 67 n

Biocosmic energy, popular belief in, 25

Bluntschli, J. K., *Allgemeines Staatesrecht,* 74

Bolsheviks and labor movement, 79

Bondurant, Joan V., applying Gandhi, 149; 146 n, 160 n

Bose, Subhas Chandra, in Japan, 141

Bracher, Karl, *Die Deutsche Diktatur,* 87, 111

Britain: economic condition thought poor, 83; Gandhi's opposition to Empire, 139, 140-41, 143

Buddhism: preached *ahiṁsā,* 124; growth of Japanese research on, 143; and nonviolent direct action, 156; and pacifism, 120, 144-45; currently reviving, 38; thirteenth century, 36

Bureaucracy: based on ability, not family, 8; collaboration with corporations and LDP, 43; exercises administrative guidance, 20; in peace organizations, 132; a phase of rationalization, 66; use of police to suppress struggle, 13; trampled human rights, 13

Censorship, prewar Japanese, 139

Christianity: a base of Japanese socialism, 77; Graeco-Roman influence on, 122; Indian religion shares features with, 51; Itō finds no equivalent in Japan, 74; monotheism a problem in Japan, 70; and nonresistance, 137; pacifist influence, 119; and Western wealth and power, 69

Citizens' movements: and alienation, 20; and nonviolent action, 159; and pollution laws, 45; weakness of, 20

Charisma: hereditary, 37; individual emperor's, an exception, 37; and modernization, 63

China: centrifugal role of family, 9; Communist, as model for Japan, 15; Confucian values in, 4-6; cul-